Veganbell's

Indian Vegan Cookbook

Hearty and Comforting Recipes for Absolute Beginners
(Dals, Curries, Breads, Desserts, and Beyond)

Neelam Pokhrel

Recipe creator at Veganbell.com

Copyright © 2023 by Neelam Pokhrel

Disclaimer : Cooking can involve risks, including burns, cuts, and other injuries.
Please use caution when preparing food. The author and publisher are not responsible for any
adverse effects or consequences that may result from the use or application of any recipes or
instructions contained in this cookbook.

Table of Contents

Pumpkin Chana Sabji - 48
Brown chickpeas are pressure-cooked with pumpkin & spices.

Matar Mushroom Masala - 50
Peas & mushrooms are cooked in spiced tomato gravy.

Baingan Bharta - 52
Eggplant (Baingan) is charred, mashed & cooked with spices.

Aloo Gobi - 54
Classic potato-cauliflower curry.

Shimla Mirch Curry - 55
Spicy & aromatic combo of bell peppers & potatoes.

Aloo Bhindi - 56
Converts okra haters into okra lovers. :)

Broccoli Curry - 57
Rich, quick & easy broccoli potato curry.

Malai Kofta - 58
Potato-tofu fried 'dumplings' (Kofta) served with creamy gravy (Malai).

Vegan Butter Chick'n - 60
Iconic butter chicken, but vegan! Made with seitan.

Tofu Special

Kadai Tofu - 62
Tofu cubes are fried in a spiced tomato-onion gravy.

Palak Tofu - 64
Spinach is cooked with cashew-tomato, then pureed & mixed w/fried tofu.

Tofu Tikka Masala - 66
Restaurant-style grilled tofu.

Golden Tofu Curry - 68
Tofu and veggie curry, enriched by coconut milk. Super versatile.

Snacks

Aloo Tikki - 69
Potato patties. Potatoes are boiled, mashed, mixed with spices, then fried.

Pyaaz Pakoda - 70
Thinly sliced onion is mixed w/chickpea flour + spices, then deep-fried.

Gobi Pakoda - 71
Cauliflower florets are marinated, dipped in batter, then deep-fried.

Samosa Pockets - 72
Savory pastry filled w/spiced potatoes.

Chatpate - 74
Super light oil-free snack made with puffed rice.

Breads

Veggie Cheela - 75
Savory Indian pancakes.

Aloo Pyaaz Paratha - 76
Potato-onion mixture is stuffed inside a flatbread dough, then cooked.

Gobi Paratha - 78
Grated cauliflower mixture is stuffed inside a flatbread dough, then cooked.

Garlic Naan - 80
Soft and fluffy bread with a delicious garlicky flavor.

Masala Dosa - 82
A fermented rice batter is cooked into a thin, flat 'crepe'.

Roti - 84

Plain flatbread made with whole wheat flour & served with veggies/curries/dals.

Desserts

Kaju Katli - 86

Sweet cashew slices. Great for parties.

Gajar Halwa - 87

Soft, sweet, and juicy pudding made from grated carrots.

Gulab Jamun - 88

Sweet potato dough is rolled into balls, fried, and soaked in syrup.

Pista Kulfi - 90

Creamy cashew-pistachio popsicle.

Mango Kulfi - 90

Mango popsicle made with cashews & coconut cream. Delicious summer treat.

Kheer - 91

Sweet & spiced rice pudding made by cooking vegan milk w/sugar + rice.

Sesame Laddoo - 92

4-ingredient dessert made with toasted sesame seeds & jaggery.

Coconut Laddoo - 93

Sweet, soft, spiced coconut bites.

Besan Laddoo - 94

Besan (Bengal gram flour) is roasted, mixed w/sugar and rolled into balls.

Banana Lassi - 95

Sweet and tangy banana smoothie.

Mango Lassi - 95

Sweet and tangy mango smoothie.

Achar & Chutney

Imli Chutney - 96

Tangy condiment made from tamarind, jaggery, and spices.

Coconut Chutney - 97

Spicy condiment made from grated coconut.

Tomato Chutney - 98

Tangy and spicy condiment made from tomato. Perfect for dips and toppings.

Mint Chutney - 99

Similar to Tomato Chutney, but made from fresh mint leaves.

Cucumber Achar - 100

Spicy & crunchy 'pickle' made from cucumber & potato.

Miscellaneous

Raita - 101

Spiced & savory condiment made with vegan yogurt. Very refreshing.

Garam Masala - 102

A blend of powdered spices and aromatics.

Masala Chai Spice - 103

A blend of powdered spices to make chai.

Masala Chai - 103

Classic Indian 'white' tea.

Paanch Furan - 104

Mixture of 5 aromatic seeds. They are fried in oil (tempered) for flavor.

Fruit Custard - 105

Creamy and fruity dessert.

Chutney Sandwich - 106

Green chutney is spread on a sandwich bread.

Introduction

Welcome to Veganbell's Indian Vegan Cookbook, a collection of plant-based recipes inspired by my childhood memories and traditional Indian cooking.

From my first attempt at making Khichdi in an old pressure cooker to discovering the wealth of flavor in dairy-free Indian cuisine, I have been on a journey to create *healthy* and delicious vegan dishes that celebrate the diverse tastes and spices of India.

With almost 30% of the Indian population following a lacto-vegetarian diet, there is a rich tradition of whole-foods cooking that emphasizes grains, beans, peas, legumes, tubers, and vegetables.

By taking dairy out of the equation, we unlock a world of flavor and nutrition that is both satisfying and sustainable.

In this cookbook, you will find a wide variety of recipes that showcase the best of Indian vegan cooking.

From sweet and sour to bitter and spicy, these dishes are designed to tantalize your taste buds and nourish your body. And with the growing popularity of Indian cuisine, you can easily find the spices and ingredients you need at your local grocery store.

So whether you are new to vegan cooking or a seasoned pro, I invite you to join me on a culinary adventure through the vibrant and flavorful world of Indian cuisine.

Let's go!

Must Have Spices

- **Aamchur** (Dried Mango Powder) is made by grinding dried raw mangoes. It's used as a souring agent in curries and soups.

- **Ajwain** (Carom Seeds) have a peculiar pungent aroma, similar to thyme or cumin. It's mostly used as 'tadka' to flavor lentils.

- **Dalchini** (Cinnamon Sticks) have a warm and woody aroma and is used in dal, tofu, spiced drinks, etc.

- **Dhaniya** (Coriander Seeds) are used predominantly in cooking veggies, curries, and soups.

- **Haldi** (Turmeric Powder) is dried & ground form of turmeric root. It has a warm, bitter flavor and gives a yellow hue to a dish.

- **Elaichi** (Cardamoms) are frequently used in sweet and savory recipes.

- **Garam Masala** is a powdered spice mix of coriander, cumin, cardamom, cloves, black pepper, cinnamon, bay leaves, and nutmeg.

- **Hing** (Asafoetida) has a unique pungent smell that adds flavor to dals and curries.

- **Imli** (Tamarind) is a sour, pulp-like, fibrous fruit that's used to prepare chutneys, curries, and soups. It's easily available in the market as Tamarind Paste.

- **Jaiphal** (Nutmeg) is a powdered spice made from the seed of a nutmeg tree. It imparts a warm and spicy flavor to a dish.

- **Jeera** (Cumin) seeds are used as a tempering agent, and its powder is used to spice up the flavor of a dish.

- **Kadi Patta** (Curry Leaves) are used as tempering ingredients. You can get fresh curry leaves from your local Indian grocery.

- **Kesar** (Saffron) is an 'exotic' spice that gives a pleasant flavor and orangish hue to a dish. It is mostly used in desserts.

- **Red Chili Powder** is prepared by drying and grinding fresh red chilies.

- **Kashmiri Red Chili Powder** is less spicy than Red Chili Powder. It gives a bright red hue to a dish.

- **Laung** (Cloves) are mildly hot spices. Whole cloves are used in 'tempering', while powdered cloves are used in spice blends like garam masala.

- **Methi** (Fenugreek Seeds & Leaves) - Dried and crushed fenugreek leaves are used at the end of the cooking process. Fenugreek seeds are almost always sautéed in hot oil until they splutter.

- **Raee** (Black Mustard Seeds) are almost always sautéed in hot oil until they splutter.

- **Teel** (Sesame Seeds) are used to make Achar (pickle). Toasted sesame seeds also make a great garnishing ingredient.

- **Tej Patta** (Bay Leaves) impart a pleasant, cinnamon-like flavor to a dish. They're not edible and discarded after cooking.

> ### Did You Know?
> Tempering is a cooking technique in which spices (cumin seeds, fenugreek seeds, mustard seeds, green chilies, etc.) are briefly fried in oil. The spices splutter and infuse flavors into the oil.

Tip Before You Shop

Powdered spices do not have high longevity, and they lose their fragrance & flavor rather quickly. So I suggest you:

1. Buy whole spices (and store them in an air-tight container).
2. Grind them in small batches when required (perhaps 1/4 cup of spice for the next 7-10 days).
3. Store the ground spices in a small air-tight container.
4. A small blender or a spice grinder will really help you out here.

Must-Have Kitchen Tools

- **Pressure Cooker :** Stovetop / Jiggle-top / Electric pressure cooker is the single most important piece of equipment when it comes to cooking Indian foods. Rice, beans, veggies – it can cook everything. More about pressure cookers in the next chapter.

- **Pans / Skillets,** which are induction & stove-top friendly, can be used to prepare a majority of sides/vegetables. A 10-inch pan (with lid) should be more than enough to get you started. It can also be used for tempering which is super useful.

- **Crepe Pan (Tawa / Dosa Griddle)** has a smaller rim that makes cooking flatbreads, naans, and parathas so much easier. If you already have a 10-inch or 12-inch skillet, you need not invest in a crepe pan.

- **Spice Grinder** is really handy while grinding dry or wet spices. You can grind cumin seeds, coriander seeds, whole cloves, cinnamon sticks, and make garam masala using a spice grinder.

- **Mortar & Pestle** are super helpful to prepare ginger-garlic paste, or to break-open cardamom pods.

A Brief Overview On Pressure Cookers

Pressure cookers are like the superheroes of Indian kitchens, helping people cook everyday staples like grains, beans, legumes, and veggies in a jiffy.

- **They make cooking easy :** For someone who doesn't have time to look after the cooking process, a pressure cooker is a life-saver. Quick-stir the spices and ingredients, pour in some liquid, seal the lid, and let the pressure do its job.

- **They're fast :** Pressure cooking in some cases reduces the cooking time of food by up to 70% compared to conventional cooking.

- **They preserve nutrition :** Several studies have shown that pressure cooking helps retain more nutrients in food compared to conventional cooking methods, such as boiling or steaming.

- **They enhance flavor** : Pressure cooking enhances the flavor of food because it requires less water than conventional cooking methods, which prevents flavor dilution. The intense pressure also allows for deeper flavor infusion into the food.

- **They're economical** : Pressure cookers are a lot more energy efficient than their counterpart kitchen appliances.

Did You Know?

There are three generations of pressure cookers:

First Generation: These are traditional pressure cookers that work by using a weighted valve that regulates the pressure and releases excess steam. They are simple in design and do not have many safety features.

Second Generation: These pressure cookers have a spring-loaded valve that regulates pressure and releases excess steam. They are generally safer and easier to use than first generation cookers.

Third Generation: These are also called electric pressure cookers. They are programmable and have a range of safety features such as automatic pressure control, temperature sensors, and timers.

Every Dal You'll Ever Need

- Toor Dal (Split Yellow Pigeon Peas)

- Kala Chana (Brown Chickpeas)

- Chana Dal (Split & Hulled Brown Chickpeas)

- Hara Mung (Green Mung Beans)

- Mung Dal (Split Yellow Mung Dal)

- Urad Beans (Whole Black Gram)

- Urad Dal (Split Black Gram)

- Masoor Sabut (Whole Brown Lentil)

- Split Red Lentils (Masoor Dal)

- Masoor Dal (Red Lentil)

- Kabuli Chana (Chickpeas)

- Sabut Matar (Whole Dried Peas)

- Lobia (Black-Eyed Peas)

- Rajma (Kidney Beans)

Pro Tip

Beans are usually consumed whole, whereas peas and lentils are consumed in different forms : whole, split, hulled (skin-removed).

Whole beans & peas like kidney beans, black-eyed peas, chickpeas, brown chickpeas require an overnight soaking for a soft texture and a reduced cooking time.

Even if you're using a pressure cooker, I highly recommend you soak whole beans and peas.

Simple Dalia Pulao

Savory breakfast made with Dalia (cracked wheat) + veggies.

Prep - 5 min.   Cook - 15 min.   Servings - 2

Ingredients

- 1 tablespoon coconut oil
- 1 cup dalia (cracked wheat)
- 1 cup green peas (fresh or frozen)
- 1 cup chopped green beans
- 1 cup chopped carrots
- 2 cups water
- 1/2 teaspoon salt (adjust to taste)
- 2 tablespoons chopped cilantro
- 1 tablespoon lemon juice

Instructions

1. Set a pan over medium heat. Add oil.

2. Once it's hot, add dalia and continuously stir-sauté for 3-4 min, or until it turns light brown.

3. Add the peas + green beans + carrots. Stir & cook for 2 minutes.

4. Add water + salt. Give it a gentle stir.

5. Cover the pan and cook for 8-10 minutes, or until the water is absorbed.

6. Sprinkle freshly chopped cilantro and drizzle lemon juice on top. Enjoy it solo, or pair it with dals and curries.

Tamarind Rice

Spiced & tangy alternative to fried rice.

Prep - 3 min.   Cook - 7 min.   Servings - 2

Ingredients

- 2 teaspoons tamarind paste
- 1/4 cup boiling water
- 1 tablespoon coconut oil
- 1/2 teaspoon mustard seeds
- 1/4 cup raw, whole peanuts
- 1 teaspoon chana dal
- 1 teaspoon urad dal
- 1 green chili, slit lengthwise
- 2 whole dried red chilies
- 8-10 fresh (or dried) curry leaves
- Pinch of asafoetida
- 1/4 teaspoon turmeric powder
- 1/2 teaspoon salt (adjust to taste)
- 1 teaspoon jaggery powder
  (or use sugar)
- 2 tablespoons water
- 3 cups cooked rice

Instructions

1. In a small bowl, mix tamarind paste + boiling water. Mix well and set aside.

2. Set a sauté pan over medium heat. Add oil. Once it's hot, add mustard seeds
   and let them splutter for 30-40 seconds. Then add peanuts + chana dal + urad dal
   Stir-sauté for 1-2 minutes.

3. Add green chili + red chilies + curry leaves + asafoetida. Mix well and cook for 2 min.

4. Stir in tamarind water. Add turmeric powder + salt + jaggery powder + water.
   Stir well and cook until the mixture thickens up a bit. Add the cooked rice.
   Mix well and serve hot.

> **Jaggery** is a traditional sweetener, made by evaporating raw, concentrated sugarcane juice until
> it solidifies. It boasts a rich brown or golden color and has a distinct, complex sweetness with a
> hint of caramel. It's readily available in any Indian or Asian grocery stores.

Fluffy rice Pilaf. Tastes best with savory sides like Dal Makhani.

Prep - 5 min.   Cook - 8 min.   Servings - 2 to 3

Ingredients

- 1.5 cups long-grain basmati rice
- 2 tablespoons coconut oil
- 2 bay leaves
- 1 cinnamon stick (around 2-inch)
- 1 black cardamom, crushed
- 3 green cardamoms, crushed
- 3 cloves
- 1/4 cup almonds, sliced
- 1/4 cup whole cashews
- 5-6 dried dates, chopped
- 2 tablespoons raisins
- 1.5 cups water
- 1.5 tablespoons sugar
- 1/2 teaspoon salt

Instructions

1. Rinse basmati rice a few times, until the water runs clear. Transfer to a bowl and add 2-3 cups of water. Soak for 20 minutes. Then drain and set aside.

2. Set your pressure cooker over medium heat. Add oil. Once it's hot, add bay leaves + cinnamon + black cardamom + green cardamoms + cloves. Stir-sauté for 30-45 sec, or until fragrant.

3. Add almonds + cashews + dates. Stir-sauté for 2 minutes over low-medium heat. Then add raisins and stir for 30 seconds.

4. Next, add the basmati rice + water + sugar + salt. Mix well. Secure the lid, and seal the knob/valve of your pressure cooker.

5. For electric pressure cooker - Press MANUAL (or PRESSURE COOK), and set the timer to 5 minutes on HIGH PRESSURE.

   For stovetop pressure cooker - Turn the heat up to high. When it reaches high pressure, lower the heat to maintain it and set the timer to 5 min.

   For jiggle-top pressure cooker - Cook over medium heat for 1 whistle.

6. Turn off the heat and allow the pressure to release naturally for 10-15 minutes Open the lid and fluff with a fork. Enjoy with dals or curries.

Veggie Pulao One-pot rice dish with a lot of veggies.

Prep - 15 min.   Cook - 15 min.   Servings - 2

Ingredients

- 1 cup basmati rice
- 2 tablespoons coconut oil
- 1/2 teaspoon cumin seeds
- 2 bay leaves
- 1 dried red chili
- 1 cinnamon stick (around 2-inch)
- 1 black cardamom, crushed
- 3 green cardamoms, crushed
- 3 cloves
- 4 black peppercorns
- 2 red onions, chopped
- 1 green chili, chopped
- 1/2 teaspoon minced ginger
- 1/2 teaspoon minced garlic
- 1 cup cauliflower florets, sliced
- 1 carrot, chopped
- 1 cup green peas (fresh or frozen)
- 1/2 cup green beans, chopped
- 1 potato, chopped
- 1 cup water
- 1/2 teaspoon salt (adjust to taste)

Instructions

1. Rinse basmati rice a few times or until the water runs clear. Transfer to a bowl and add 3 cups of water. Soak for 20 min. After 20 min. Drain and set aside.

2. Set your electric / stovetop / jiggle-top pressure cooker over medium heat. Add oil. Once it's hot, add cumin seeds + bay leaves + dried red chili + cinnamon stick + cardamoms + cloves + peppercorns. Stir-sauté for 1 min.

3. Next, add onion + green chili. Mix well and cook for 3-4 min, or until the onion turns golden brown. Then Add ginger and garlic. Stir and cook for 1 min.

4. Add cauliflower + carrots + peas + beans + potatoes. Stir-sauté for 2-3 min, or until the veggies are lightly sautéed. Then add rice + water + salt. Give it a gentle stir.

5. Secure the lid, and seal the knob/valve of your pressure cooker.

6. <u>For electric pressure cooker</u> - Press MANUAL (or PRESSURE COOK) and set the timer to 5 min on HIGH PRESSURE.

   <u>For stovetop pressure cooker</u> - Turn the heat up to high. When it reaches high pressure, lower the heat to maintain it and set the timer to 5 min.

   <u>For jiggle-top pressure cooker</u> - Cook over medium heat for 1 whistle.

7. Turn off the heat and allow the pressure to release naturally for 10-15 min. Open the lid and gently fluff the pulao using a fork. Let it rest for 2 min. Veggie pulao is done.

Jeera Rice Leftover rice is fried with cumin + spices.

Prep - 2 min.   Cook - 5 min.   Servings - 2

Ingredients

- 4 cups cooked / leftover rice (at room temperature)
- 2 tablespoons coconut oil
- 2 dried red chilies
- 2 teaspoons cumin seeds
- 3 green cardamoms
- 3 cloves
- 1 bay leaf
- 1 cinnamon stick (2-inch piece)
- 1/2 teaspoon salt (adjust to taste)

Instructions

1. Set a pan over medium heat and add oil.
2. Once it's hot, add red chilies + cumin seeds + cardamoms + cloves + bay leaf + cinnamon stick.
3. Stir and sauté for 1 minute, or until the cumin seeds turn brown.
4. Add cooked rice and salt. Mix well and stir-cook for 4 minutes.
5. Jeera rice is ready. Enjoy with your favorite dal or curry.

Curried Beaten Rice

Light and savory breakfast made with flatten rice.

Prep - 10 min.   Cook - 10 min.   Servings - 2

Ingredients

- 2 cups beaten rice (poha)
- 1 tablespoon coconut oil
- 1/2 teaspoon mustard seeds
- 1/2 teaspoon cumin seeds
- 6-8 fresh/dried curry leaves
- 1 green chili, sliced
- 1 onion, chopped
- 1-inch ginger, chopped
- 1/2 cup finely diced carrots
- 1/2 cup green peas (fresh/frozen)
- 1/4 teaspoon turmeric powder
- 1/4 teaspoon red chili powder
- 2 tablespoons water
- 1/2 teaspoon salt
- 1 teaspoon powdered sugar
- 1/4 cup toasted peanuts

- 1/4 cup pomegranate seeds
- 1 tablespoon lemon juice
- Freshly chopped cilantro, handful

Instructions

1. Place beaten rice on a large strainer and run water through it. Rest the strainer on a bowl to remove excess water (do not squeeze). Set aside.

2. Set a pan over medium heat. Add oil. Once it's hot, add mustard seeds + cumin seeds. Let them splutter for 30-40 seconds. Then add the curry leaves + green chili. Stir and sauté for 15 seconds.

3. Now add onion + ginger and stir-sauté for 2-3 min, or until the onions become translucent. Then add carrots + peas and stir-sauté for 3 minutes.

4. Next, add turmeric powder + red chili powder. Stirring continuously, cook for 2 minutes. Add 2 tablespoons of water to prevent the masala from burning.

5. Turn down the heat to low and add beaten rice + salt + sugar + toasted peanuts. Mix well and turn off the heat. Add pomegranate seeds and drizzle lemon juice on top. Garnish with freshly chopped cilantro and serve.

Tomato Upma

Fluffy and tangy semolina porridge.

Prep - 5 min.   Cook - 20 min.   Servings - 2 to 3

Ingredients

- 1 cup semolina flour (sooji)
- 2 tablespoons coconut oil
- 1 teaspoon mustard seeds
- 1 teaspoon cumin seeds
- 1 tablespoon chana dal
- 8-10 whole cashews
- 1 green chili, chopped
- 1-inch ginger, finely chopped
- 1 medium onion, finely chopped
- 8-10 fresh/dried curry leaves
- Pinch of asafoetida (hing)
- 3 medium tomatoes, chopped
- 1/2 cup fresh or frozen green peas
- 1/4 teaspoon turmeric powder
- 1/4 tsp Kashmiri red chili powder
- 1/2 teaspoon salt (adjust to taste)
- 1/2 teaspoon sugar
- 3 cups water

Instructions

Step A : Dry-roast semolina

1. Set a pan over low-medium heat. Add semolina and dry-roast until fragrant, around 4-5 minutes. Do not brown.

2. Transfer the roasted semolina to a bowl and set aside.

Step B : Prepare the tempering

3. Set the pan over medium heat. Add oil. Once it's hot, add mustard + cumin seeds and let them splutter for 30-40 seconds.

4. Add chana dal + cashews & stir-sauté until they're golden (~2 min).

5. Now add green chili + ginger + onion + curry leaves + asafoetida. Stir-sauté for
    2 minutes.

6. Next, add tomatoes + green peas + turmeric powder + Kashmiri red chili powder +
    salt + sugar. Mix well, cover the pan, and cook for 5-6 min, or until the tomatoes
    soften.

7. Stir in water. Turn up the heat to high and bring it to a boil.

Step C : Mix well & cook the Upma

8. Turn down the heat to low and gradually add the roasted semolina, while
    continuously stirring the mixture to prevent any lumps.

9. Cover the pan and cook over low- medium heat for 2-3 minutes, or until the liquid is
    completely absorbed. Tomato upma is ready. Serve hot.

Idli   Savory rice cake made by steaming a fermented batter of rice + lentil.

Prep - 20 hr.   Cook - 12 min.   Servings - 3 to 4

Ingredients

- 1.5 cups Idli rice or parboiled rice (or use Basmati rice)
- 1/2 cup Urad dal (split & dehusked black gram)
- 1/4 teaspoon Fenugreek seeds
- 1.5 cups Water, to blend
- Salt, to taste

Instructions

Step A: Soak rice and dal

1. Rinse the rice until the water runs clear. Transfer it to a large bowl and add 3 cups of water. Soak overnight. In a separate bowl, add urad dal + fenugreek seeds. Soak overnight.

Step B: Blend

2. Once the rice and dal are soaked, drain the rice and divide it into 2 equal batches.

3. Transfer 1 batch to a grinder/blender along with 1/2 cup water. Blend it to a fine mixture. Remove it to a bowl and set aside. Repeat the same for the remaining batch.

4. Next, drain the urad dal mixture and transfer it to the grinder/blender. Add 1/2 cup water & blend until smooth. Combine and mix the rice and urad dal mixtures together.

Step C: Ferment

5. Cover and set aside in a warm place for at least 12 hours[*] and allow the batter to ferment. A fermented batter will have a slightly increased volume and thicker & fluffier texture.

6. After 12 hours, add 2 to 3 tablespoons water + salt to the thick fermented batter. Give it a gentle stir.

7. You can steam the idli using 3 different methods:

Method 1 - Using an Idli Mould

- Fill an idli steamer or a large pot with about 1-2 inches of water. Bring it to a boil.
- Grease the idli moulds with a little oil to prevent the idli from sticking.
- Pour the idli batter into each of the moulds, filling them about 3/4th full.
- Place the filled idli moulds into the steamer or pot, ensure the water does not touch the bottom of the moulds.
- Cover with a lid and steam for about 10-12 minutes on medium heat.
- To check if the idlis are done, insert a toothpick in the center of an idli. If it comes out clean, they're ready.
- Remove the mould from the steamer and let it sit for a few minutes. Then, use a spoon to remove the idlis from the moulds.

Method 2- Using a Small Steel Bowl and a Steamer Basket

- If you don't have an idli mould, you can use a small steel bowl and a steamer basket. Follow the same steps as above, but instead of pouring the batter into the idli moulds, pour it into the greased steel bowls.
- Place the bowls in a steamer basket and steam for 15-20 min on medium heat, or until a toothpick inserted in the center comes out clean.
- Once done, let it cool for a few minutes, then invert the bowl to remove the idli.

Method 3- Using a Microwave

- If you prefer to use a microwave, pour the idli batter into a microwave-safe bowl or silicone idli moulds.
- Microwave on high for about 1-2 minutes, or until a toothpick inserted in the center comes out clean. Be sure to check the idli after 1 minute and then microwave for additional time if needed.
- Let the idli cool for a couple of minutes before removing from the mould.

8. Idli is ready! Enjoy with coconut chutney, sambar, or your fav dal.

> **Note**
>
> *   It may take longer than 12 hours for the batter to ferment if the ambient temperature is low.

   3 types of lentils are first cooked then simmered with spices.
Prep - 5 min.   Cook - 15 min.   Servings - 2 to 3

Ingredients

To cook dals:

- 1/4 cup masoor dal (red lentils)
- 1/4 cup mung dal
  (split yellow mung beans)
- 1/2 cup toor dal / arhar dal
  (split yellow pigeon peas)
- 2.5 cups water
- 1/2 teaspoon salt (adjust to taste)
- 1/4 teaspoon turmeric powder

To prepare tadka:

- 1 tablespoon coconut oil
- 1/2 teaspoon cumin seeds
- 3 garlic cloves, chopped
- 1/2 inch ginger, chopped
- 1 green chili, chopped
- 1 onion, chopped
- Pinch of asafoetida
- 1/4 tsp Kashmiri red chili powder
- 1 tomato, chopped

To garnish:

- 2 tablespoons chopped cilantro

Instructions

Step A : Cook Dals

1. Rinse all three dals and transfer them to your pressure cooker. Add water + salt + turmeric powder.

2. For electric pressure cooker - Secure the lid, seal the knob, press MANUAL (or PRESSURE COOK) & set the timer to 7 minutes on HIGH PRESSURE. Let the pressure release naturally for 8-10 minutes.

For stovetop pressure cooker - Secure the lid, seal the valve, turn the heat up to high and when the cooker indicates it has reached high pressure, lower the heat to maintain it and begin counting 7 minutes pressure cooking time. Turn off the heat and allow the pressure to release naturally for 8- 10 minutes.

For jiggle-top pressure cooker - Secure the lid, put the whistle on, and cook over medium heat for 6-7 whistles. Note: As some liquid escapes from the jiggle-top cooker, you can add an additional 1/2 cup water prior to cooking. Turn off the heat and allow the pressure to release naturally for 8- 10 minutes.

Step B : Prepare the tadka

3. Heat a frying pan/skillet over medium heat. Add oil. Once it's hot, add cumin seeds and let it splutter for 30-40 sec.

4. Add ginger + garlic + green chili + onion + asafoetida. Stir and sauté for 3-4 min, or until the onion is golden.

5. Add Kashmiri red chili powder + tomato. Mix well and cook for 3-4 min, or until the tomato gets mushy.

6. Turn off the heat and transfer the tadka to the pressure cooker.

7. Mix well. Add a splash of water.

8. Set your pressure cooker over medium heat and bring it to a simmer. Turn off the heat. Adjust salt and sprinkle freshly chopped cilantro. Mix well.
    Dal tadka is ready.

Dal Makhani   Creamy and buttery dal made with urad & kidney beans.

Prep - 5 min.   Cook - 55 min.   Servings - 2 to 3

Ingredients

To soak the lentils,

- 1 cup urad beans (whole black gram)
- 1/4 cup rajma (kidney beans)
- 4 cups of water

To pressure cook,

- 3 cloves
- 3 green cardamoms
- 1 black cardamom
- 1 bay leaf
- 1 cinnamon stick
- 1/2 teaspoon salt
- 3 cups of water

To prepare the masala,

- 2 tablespoons coconut oil
- 1 onion, roughly chopped
- 3 garlic cloves
- 1-inch ginger
- 2 tablespoons water
- 1 cup blended tomatoes
- 1/2 teaspoon turmeric powder
- 1/2 teaspoon Kashmiri red chili powder
- 1/2 teaspoon coriander powder
- 1/2 teaspoon cumin powder
- 1/2 teaspoon salt (adjust to taste)
- 1/2 cup coconut cream
- 2 tablespoons vegan butter

Instructions

Step A : Soak the beans

1. Rinse urad beans + kidney beans. Transfer to a large bowl and add 4 cups of water. Soak overnight.

2. Drain the soaked lentils and transfer them to your pressure cooker.

3. Add cloves + green cardamoms + black cardamom + cinnamon stick + bay leaf + salt + 3 cups of water.

4. For electric pressure cooker - Secure the lid, seal the knob, press MANUAL (or PRESSURE COOK) and set the timer to 25 min on HIGH PRESSURE. Let the pressure release naturally for 10-15 min.

    For stovetop pressure cooker - Secure the lid, seal the valve, turn the heat up to high and when the cooker indicates it has reached high pressure, lower the heat to maintain it and begin counting 25 min pressure cooking time.
    Turn off the heat and allow the pressure to release naturally for 10-15 min.

    For jiggle-top pressure cooker - Secure the lid, put the whistle on, and cook over medium heat for 7-8 whistles. Note: As some of the liquid escapes from the jiggle-top cooker, you can add an additional 1/2 cup water prior to cooking. Turn off the heat and allow the pressure to release naturally for 10-15 minutes.

5. Open the lid and check the kidney beans for doneness. If they're not super soft and mushy, cook for 5 more minutes using the same heat settings.
    For a creamier consistency, mash 1/4 portion of the dal or blend them.

6. Transfer everything to a large bowl and quick-rinse your pressure cooker.

Step C : Temper the masala

7. In a blender, add onion + garlic + ginger + 2 tablespoons water. Blend to make a paste. Set aside.

8. Set your electric pressure cooker to SAUTE (or set your stovetop / jiggletop pressure cooker over medium heat). Add oil. Once it's hot, add onion-garlic paste. Stir and sauté for 8-9 minutes, or until the paste turns brown.

9. Next, add blended tomatoes + turmeric powder + Kashmiri red chili powder + cumin powder + coriander powder + salt. Mix well and cook for 12-15 minutes, or until most of the liquid evaporates and the oil separates from the mixture. Stir frequently.

10. Stir in the cooked dal + 1 cup water and bring it to a boil. For a thicker consistency, let it simmer for 5-6 min.

11. Turn off the heat. Add coconut cream + vegan butter + cilantro. Give it a gentle stir. Dal makhani is ready. Serve hot with rice, roti, naan, or pulao.

 Chickpeas are cooked and simmered in a spicy tomato gravy.

Prep - 8 min.   Cook - 40 min.   Servings - 3

Ingredients

To soak,

- 1 cup kabuli chana (chickpeas)
- 4 cups water

To prepare 'tea',

- 1 cup water
- 1.5 teaspoon loose tea leaves

To pressure cook,

- 1 black cardamom
- 3 green cardamoms
- 3 cloves
- 1 cinnamon stick
- 1 bay leaf
- 1/2 teaspoon salt (adjust to taste)
- 2 cups water

To prepare masala,

- 2 tablespoons cooking oil
- 2 medium onions, chopped
- 1 tablespoon ginger-garlic paste
- 1 cup blended tomatoes
- 1/4 teaspoon turmeric powder
- 1 teaspoon Kashmiri red chili powder
- 1 teaspoon coriander powder
- 1/2 teaspoon cumin powder
- 1 teaspoon amchur (dried mango powder)
- 2 cups water
- 1/2 teaspoon garam masala
- 1/2 teaspoon kasuri methi
  (dried fenugreek leaves, optional)

To garnish,

- 1/4 cup freshly chopped cilantro

Instructions

Step A : Soak the chickpeas

1. Rinse chickpeas and transfer to a bowl. Add 4 cups of water. Soak overnight.

Step B : Prepare the 'tea'

2. In a saucepan, boil water with loose tea leaves. Strain and set aside.

Step C : Pressure-cook

3. To your electric / stovetop / jiggle-top pressure cooker, add soaked chickpeas + tea + black cardamom + green cardamoms + cloves + cinnamon stick + bay leaf + salt + water.

4. For electric pressure cooker - Secure the lid, seal the knob, press MANUAL (or PRESSURE COOK) and set the timer to 15 min. on HIGH PRESSURE. Let the pressure release naturally for 10-15 min.

   For stovetop pressure cooker - Secure the lid, seal the valve, turn the heat up to high and when the cooker indicates it has reached high pressure, lower the heat to maintain it and begin counting 15 minutes pressure cooking time. Turn off the heat and allow the pressure to release naturally for 10-15 minutes.

   For jiggle-top pressure cooker - Secure the lid, put the whistle on, and cook over medium heat for 5-6 whistles. Turn off the heat & allow the pressure to release naturally for 10-15 minutes.

5. Open the lid and gently mash around 1 cup of the cooked chickpeas. This will make the dish creamier.

Step D : Prepare the masala

6. Transfer everything to a large bowl and give your pressure cooker a quick rinse.

7. Set your pressure cooker over medium heat. Add oil. Once it's hot, add onion and stir-sauté for 3-4 min, or until brown. Add ginger-garlic paste. Stir and cook for 2 minutes, or until the raw garlicky aroma disappears.

8. Add blended tomatoes + salt + turmeric powder + Kashmiri red chili powder + coriander powder + cumin powder + amchur. Stir and cook for 12 to 15 minutes, or until most of the liquid evaporates and the oil separates from the mixture.

9. Add cooked chickpeas + water. Bring it to a boil and simmer for 5 minutes.

10. Turn off the heat. Add garam masala + kasuri methi. Mix well. Garnish with freshly chopped cilantro and serve with rice or roti.

Rajma Chawal

Kidney beans are cooked in a masala gravy & served w/rice.

Prep - 5 min.   Cook - 50 min.   Servings - 2 to 3

Ingredients

To soak kidney beans,

- 1 cup kidney beans
- 4 cups water

To pressure-cook,

- 1 bay leaf
- 1 black cardamom
- 3 green cardamoms
- 3 cloves
- 1 cinnamon stick
- 1/2 teaspoon salt
- 2 cups water

To blend the tomatoes,

- 4 medium tomatoes, quartered
- 2 green chilies, halved
- 2-inch piece ginger, halved
- 4 garlic cloves

To prepare gravy/masala,

- 2 tablespoons oil
- 1/2 teaspoon cumin seeds
- 1 red onion, chopped
- 1/2 teaspoon turmeric powder
- 1 teaspoon coriander powder
- 1 teaspoon cumin powder
- 1/2 teaspoon amchur (dried mango powder)
- 1/2 tsp Kashmiri red chili powder
- 1/2 teaspoon salt (adjust to taste)
- 1/4 teaspoon pepper
- 1/2 teaspoon garam masala
- 1/4 cup freshly chopped cilantro

Instructions

Step A : Soak the kidney beans

1. Rinse and transfer kidney beans to a bowl. Add 4 cups of water and soak overnight.

Step B : Pressure cook

2. In your electric / stovetop / jiggle-top pressure cooker, add soaked (and drained) kidney beans + bay leaf + black cardamom + green cardamoms + cloves + cinnamon stick + salt + water.

3. For electric pressure cooker - Secure the lid, seal the knob, press MANUAL (or PRESSURE COOK) and set the timer to 25 min on HIGH PRESSURE. Let the pressure release naturally for 10-15 min.

   For stovetop pressure cooker - Secure the lid, seal the valve, turn the heat up to high and when the cooker indicates it has reached high pressure, lower the heat to maintain it and begin counting 25 minutes pressure cooking time. Turn off the heat and allow the pressure to release naturally for 10-15 min.

   For jiggle-top pressure cooker - NOTE: As much of the liquid escapes from the jiggle-top cooker, you need to add an additional 1 cup water prior to cooking rajma. Then secure the lid, put the whistle on, and cook over medium heat for 7-8 whistles. Turn off the heat and allow the pressure to release naturally for 10-15 min.

Step C : Prepare the gravy

4. In a blender, blend tomatoes + green chilies + ginger + garlic to a fine puree. Set aside.

5. Set a pan over medium heat. Add oil. Once it's hot, add cumin seeds and let it splutter for 30-40 seconds. Then add onion & stir-sauté for 3-4 min, or until golden brown.

6. Add pureed tomato + turmeric powder + coriander powder + cumin powder + amchur + Kashmiri red chili powder + salt + pepper. Stir and mix.

7. Cook for 12-15 min, or until most of the liquid evaporates and the oil separates from the mixture. Stir frequently.

Step D : Mix cooked kidney beans with the gravy

8. Transfer the gravy to your pressure cooker and add garam masala. Stir and mix well. Put the lid on (do not seal) and simmer for 4-5 min. Add a splash of water if needed.

9. Turn off the heat, garnish with freshly chopped cilantro, adjust salt, and serve over basmati rice.

Lobia Dal

Spiced lobia (black-eyed peas) dal.

Prep - 5 min.   Cook - 20 min.   Servings - 2 to 3

Ingredients

- 1 cup black-eyed peas (lobia), rinsed
- 1.5 tablespoons coconut oil
- 1/2 teaspoon cumin seeds
- 1 large onion, chopped
- 1-inch ginger, finely chopped
- 4 garlic cloves, finely chopped
- 2 green chilies, slit lengthwise
- 3 medium tomatoes, chopped
- 1/2 teaspoon salt (adjust to taste)
- 1/4 teaspoon turmeric powder
- 1/2 tsp Kashmiri red chili powder
- 1 teaspoon coriander powder
- 1/2 teaspoon cumin powder
- 3 cups water
- 1/2 tsp garam masala powder
- 1/4 cup freshly chopped cilantro

Instructions

Step A : Soak

1. Add (lobia) black-eyed peas + 4 cups of water in a large mixing bowl. Soak overnight. Drain and set aside.

Step B : Prepare the masala

2. Set your electric / stovetop / jiggle-top pressure cooker over medium heat. Add oil. Once it's hot, add cumin seeds and let it splutter for 30-40 sec. Next, add onion and stir-sauté for 3-4 minutes, or until golden.

3. Add ginger + garlic + green chilies and stir-sauté for 1-2 minutes, or until the raw garlicky aroma disappears.

4. Add tomatoes + salt + turmeric + Kashmiri red chili powder + coriander powder + cumin powder. Mix well.

5. Cover the cooker (do not seal) & cook for 3-4 min, or until the tomatoes are soft and mushy. Stir occasionally.

Step C : Pressure cook

6. Next, add the soaked (and drained) black-eyed peas to the cooker.

7. Mix well and cook for 2-3 minutes. Add water and give it a good stir.

8. For electric pressure cooker - Secure the lid, seal the knob, press MANUAL (or PRESSURE COOK) and set the timer to 10 min on HIGH PRESSURE. Let the pressure release naturally for 10-15 min.

    For stovetop pressure cooker - Secure the lid, seal the pressure valve, turn the heat up to high and when the cooker indicates it has reached high pressure, lower the heat to maintain it and begin counting 10 min pressure cooking time. Turn off the heat & allow the pressure to release naturally for 10- 15 min.

    For jiggle-top pressure cooker - Secure the lid, put the whistle on, and cook over medium heat for 5-6 whistles. Let the pressure release naturally for 10-15 min.

9. Open the lid and add garam masala + freshly chopped cilantro. You can also mash a portion of the lobia for a thicker consistency. Mix well and serve hot.

Urad Dal Tadka

Spices are fried and cooked with urad beans.

Prep - 5 min.   Cook - 25 min.   Servings - 3 to 4

Ingredients

- 1 cup urad beans (whole black gram)
- 5 cups water
- 1/4 teaspoon turmeric powder
- 1/2 teaspoon salt (adjust to taste)
- 1/2 tsp Kashmiri red chili powder
- 1 teaspoon coriander powder
- 1/2 teaspoon amchur
  (dried mango powder)
- 1 green chili, chopped
- 1-inch ginger, chopped
- 1.5 tablespoons coconut oil
- 1 teaspoon cumin seeds
- 1/2 teaspoon mustard seeds
- 1 cinnamon stick
- 2 black cardamoms
- 1 large bay leaf
- 3 cloves
- 2 dried red chilies (whole)
- 1/2 teaspoon saunf (fennel seeds)
- Pinch of asafoetida
- 1 tsp dried fenugreek leaves
- 1/2 teaspoon garam masala
- 1/4 cup freshly chopped cilantro
- 1 tablespoon lemon juice

Step A : Cook the lentils

1. Rinse and transfer urad beans to your electric/stovetop/jiggle-top cooker. Add water + turmeric powder + salt.

2. For electric pressure cooker - Secure the lid, seal the knob, press MANUAL (or PRESSURE COOK) and set the timer to 12 min on HIGH PRESSURE. Let the pressure release naturally for 10-15 min.

   For stovetop pressure cooker - Secure lid, seal the pressure valve, turn the heat up to high and when the cooker indicates it has reached high pressure, lower the heat to maintain it and begin counting 12 min pressure cooking time. Let the pressure release naturally for 10-15 minutes.

   For jiggle-top pressure cooker - Secure the lid, put the whistle on, and cook over medium heat for 6-7 whistles. Let the pressure release naturally for 10-15 minutes.

3. Open the lid, add Kashmiri red chili powder + coriander powder + amchur + green chili + ginger to the cooked lentil. Mix well, bring it to a boil and let it simmer for 2 min.

Step B : Prepare the tadka

4. Set a sauté pan over medium heat. Add oil. Once it's hot, add cumin seeds + mustard seeds + cinnamon stick + cardamoms + bay leaf + cloves + dried red chilies + fennel seeds.

5. Stir and sauté for 1-2 min. Next, add asafoetida and stir-cook for 10-15 seconds.

Step C : Mix lentil and tadka

6. Pour tadka over the cooked lentils.

7. Add dried fenugreek leaves + garam masala. Mix well and garnish with freshly chopped cilantro and lemon juice.

   Goodness of spinach and lentil in a bowl.

Prep - 5 min.   Cook - 15 min.   Servings - 2 to 3

Ingredients

- 1/4 cup toor dal / arhar dal
  (split yellow pigeon peas)

- 1/4 cup masoor dal (split red lentils)

- 2.5 cups water

- 1/4 teaspoon turmeric powder

- 1/2 teaspoon salt (adjust to taste)

- 1.5 tablespoons coconut oil

- 1/2 teaspoon cumin seeds

- 1-inch ginger, chopped

- 1 green chili, chopped

- Pinch of asafoetida

- 3.5 oz. (100 gm.) baby spinach,
  chopped

- 1/4 teaspoon roasted cumin powder

- 1/4 teaspoon Kashmiri red chili powder

Instructions

Step A : Cook the lentils

1. Rinse and transfer dals to your pressure cooker. Add water + turmeric powder + salt.

2. For electric pressure cooker - Secure the lid, seal the knob, press MANUAL (or PRESSURE COOK) and set the timer to 7 min on HIGH PRESSURE. Let the pressure release naturally for 8-10 minutes.

   For stovetop pressure cooker - Secure the lid, seal the pressure valve, turn the heat up to high and when the cooker indicates it has reached high pressure, lower the heat to maintain it and begin counting 7 min pressure cooking time. Turn off the heat & allow the pressure to release naturally for 8- 10 min.

For jiggle-top pressure cooker - Secure the lid, put the whistle on, and cook over medium heat for 4-5 whistles. Let the pressure release naturally for 8-10 min.

Step B : Sauté the spinach

3. Set a sauté pan over medium heat. Add oil.

4. Once it's hot, add the cumin seeds and let them splutter for 30-40 seconds.

5. Add ginger + green chili + asafoetida and sauté for 1 minute.

6. Next, add spinach + roasted cumin powder + red chili powder. Stir- cook for 2-3 minutes, or until the spinach is soft and wilted.

Step C : Mix lentil and spinach

7. Once the spinach is wilted, transfer it to the pressure cooker. Mix well. Adjust salt and let it simmer for 2-3 minutes. Serve hot.

Chana Dal Fry

A spiced tomato gravy is simmered with cooked chana dal.

Prep - 5 min.   Cook - 20 min.   Servings - 2 to 3

Ingredients

To pressure-cook,

- 1 cup chana dal (split Bengal gram)
- 3 cups water
- 1/4 teaspoon turmeric powder
- 1/2 teaspoon salt
- 1 bay leaf

To prepare tadka,

- 1.5 tablespoons coconut oil
- 1/2 teaspoon cumin seeds
- 1-inch ginger, chopped
- 4 garlic cloves, chopped
- 1 whole dried red chili
- Pinch of asafoetida
- 2 onions, chopped
- 1 green chili, slit lengthwise
- 1 large tomato, chopped
- 1/2 teaspoon salt (adjust to taste)
- 1/2 teaspoon Kashmiri red chili powder
- 1/2 teaspoon cumin powder
- 1/2 teaspoon coriander powder
- 1/4 cup freshly chopped cilantro

Instructions

Step A : Pressure-cook

1. Rinse & soak chana dal for 1 hour.

2. Drain and transfer to your pressure cooker. Add water + turmeric powder + salt + bay leaf. Stir well.

3. For electric pressure cooker - Secure the lid, seal the knob, press MANUAL (or PRESSURE COOK) and set the timer to 10 min on HIGH PRESSURE. Let the pressure release naturally for 8-10 min.

For stovetop pressure cooker - Secure the lid, seal the valve, turn the heat up to high and when the cooker indicates it has reached high pressure, lower the heat to maintain it and begin counting 10 min pressure cooking time. Let the pressure release naturally for 8-10 minutes.

For jiggle-top pressure cooker - NOTE: As much of the liquid escapes from the jiggle-top cooker, you need to add an additional 1/2 cup water prior to cooking the chana. Then secure the lid, put the whistle on, and cook over medium heat for 5-6 whistles. Let the pressure release naturally for 8-10 min.

Step B : Prepare the tadka

4. Set a sauté pan over medium heat. Add oil. Once it's hot, add cumin seeds and let them splutter for 20-30 seconds.

5. Then add ginger + garlic + dried red chili + asafoetida + onion + green chili. Stir-sauté for 3-4 min, or until the onion is golden.

6. Next, add tomato + salt + Kashmiri red chili powder + cumin powder + coriander powder. Mix well, turn down the heat to medium, and cook for 3-4 min, or until the tomato is soft & mushy (stir occasionally).

Step C : Mix chana dal and tadka

7. Add the prepared tadka to the pressure cooker. Mix well and bring it to a boil. Turn off the heat, garnish with freshly chopped cilantro, and serve hot.

Yellow Peas Dal

Rich and creamy dal made with dried peas and potatoes.

Prep - 7 min.   Cook - 20 min.   Servings - 3 to 4

Ingredients

- 1 cup whole dried yellow peas
- 1.5 tablespoons oil
- 1 medium onion, sliced
- 2 medium potatoes, diced
- 1.5 tablespoon ginger-garlic paste
- 1/4 teaspoon turmeric powder
- 1/2 teaspoon cumin powder
- 1/2 teaspoon coriander powder
- 1/2 teaspoon Kashmiri chili powder
- 2 large tomatoes, chopped
- 1/2 teaspoon salt (adjust to taste)
- 3 cups water
- 1/4 cup freshly chopped cilantro

Instructions

Step A : Soak the peas

1. Rinse and transfer the peas to a large bowl. Add 3 cups of water. Soak overnight.

Step B : Prepare the masala

2. Heat up your pressure cooker. Add oil. Once it's hot, add onion and stir-sauté for 3-4 min, or until golden. Add potatoes and stir-sauté for 3 min.

3. Now, add the (soaked & drained) peas + ginger-garlic paste + turmeric powder + cumin powder + coriander powder + Kashmiri red chili powder + tomatoes + salt.

4. Stirring well, scrape off any brown bits from the bottom of the cooker.
   Cook for 3-4 min, or until the tomatoes are softened. Add water and stir well.

5. For electric pressure cooker -Secure the lid, seal the knob, press MANUAL (or PRESSURE COOK) and set the timer to 10 min on HIGH PRESSURE. Let the pressure release naturally for 10-15 min.

   For stovetop pressure cooker - Secure the lid, seal the pressure valve, turn the heat up to high and when the cooker indicates it has reached high pressure, lower the heat to maintain it for 10 minutes. Turn off the heat. Natural release for 10-15 minutes.

   For jiggle-top pressure cooker - Secure the lid, put the whistle on, and cook over medium heat for 5-6 whistles. Note: As some of the liquid escapes from the jiggle-top cooker, you can add an additional 1/2 cup water prior to cooking. Turn off the heat and allow the pressure to release naturally for 10 - 12 minutes.

6. Open the lid and lightly mash the potatoes. Sprinkle freshly chopped cilantro.

7. Mix well and serve hot with rice, roti, naan, or your fav bread.

Curried Coconut Dal

Pan-cooked red lentils. Enriched with coconut milk.

Prep - 7 min.   Cook - 18 min.   Servings - 2 to 3

Ingredients

- 2 tablespoons coconut oil
- 1 red onion, chopped
- 1-inch piece ginger, finely chopped
- 4 garlic cloves, finely chopped
- 1/2 teaspoon cumin powder
- 1/2 teaspoon coriander powder
- 1/4 teaspoon turmeric powder
- 1/4 teaspoon Kashmiri chili powder
- 2 cups water
- 1 cup coconut milk
- 1 cup masoor dal (split red lentils)
- 1 carrot, sliced
- 1/2 teaspoon salt (adjust to taste)
- 1/4 cup freshly chopped cilantro
- 1 tablespoon lemon juice

Instructions

1. Rinse and soak masoor dal for 20 min.
   NOTE: Soaking is optional, but it will considerably lessen the cooking time.

2. Set a thick-bottomed pan over medium heat. Add oil. Once it's hot, add onion and stir-sauté for 3-4 min, or until it's golden.

3. Add ginger + garlic and stir-sauté for 1 min, or until the raw garlicky aroma disappears. Next, add cumin powder + coriander powder + turmeric powder + Kashmiri red chili powder. Stir & cook for 1 min.

4. Stir in water + coconut milk + (drained) lentils + carrot + salt. Cover the pan and cook over medium heat for 10-12 min, stirring occasionally. Unsoaked lentils take 19-22 min to cook.

5. Turn off the heat. Garnish with freshly chopped cilantro. Drizzle lemon juice and give it a gentle stir. Serve hot.

Hearty one-pot meal made with quinoa and mung dal.

Prep - 10 min.   Cook - 45 min.   Servings - 2 to 3

Ingredients

- 1 cup quinoa
- 1/2 cup mung dal
- 2 tablespoons oil
- 1 teaspoon mustard seeds
- 1 teaspoon cumin seeds
- 1 onion, chopped
- 1 inch ginger, finely chopped
- 3 cloves garlic, finely chopped
- 2 green chilies, finely chopped
- 1/4 teaspoon asafoetida (hing)
- 3 tomatoes, chopped
- 1/2 teaspoon turmeric powder
- 1/2 tsp Kashmiri red chili powder
- Salt
- 1 cup chopped green beans
- 1 cup chopped carrots
- 1 cup green peas
- 5 cups water
- 2 tablespoons lemon juice
- 1/4 cup freshly chopped cilantro
- Vegan butter (to garnish - optional)

Instructions

1. Wash quinoa + mung dal and transfer them to a large bowl. Add 3-4 cups of hot water. Soak for 30 minutes. *After 30 minutes* Drain and set aside.

2. Set a large, non-stick cooking pot over medium heat. Add oil. Once it's hot, add mustard seeds + cumin seeds. Stir and let them splutter for 30-40 seconds, or until the cumin seeds are dark brown.

3. Add onion + ginger + garlic + green chilies + asafoetida. Stir-sauté for 3-4 minutes, or until the onion is translucent.

4. Next, add tomatoes + turmeric powder + Kashmiri red chili powder + salt. Stir-sauté for 5-6 minutes, or until the tomatoes are completely mushy.

5. Now add the quinoa & mung dal + green beans + carrots + green peas + water. Mix well. Cover the pot and cook over low-medium heat for 30-35 minutes. Stir occasionally (every 8-9 minutes).

6. Once it's done, add lemon juice + cilantro. Give it a quick mix. Turn off the heat.

7. Transfer to serving bowls and garnish with a dollop of vegan butter (optional). Enjoy!

Sambar   Tangy south Indian staple soup Made with lentils + mixed veggies.

Prep - 15 min.   Cook - 40 min.   Servings - 3

Ingredients

To soak the lentils,

- 1/4 cup toor/arhar dal
- 1 cup water
- To prepare tamarind water,
- 2 teaspoons tamarind paste
- 1/4 cup warm water

To prepare sambar masala,
Note: You can also buy readymade Sambar Masala (and skip this step)

- 1 tablespoon oil
- 1/2 teaspoon cumin seeds
- 1/2 teaspoon coriander seeds
- 1/8 teaspoon fenugreek seeds
- 1 tablespoon chana dal
- Pinch of asafoetida
- 4 cloves
- 1 green cardamom
- 1 medium onion, sliced
- 1-inch ginger, chopped
- 5 garlic cloves, chopped
- 2 whole dried red chilies
- 1/4 teaspoon turmeric powder

- 1 tsp Kashmiri red chili powder
- 1/2 teaspoon salt
- 1/4 cup water

To prepare sambar,

- 1 tablespoon oil
- 1 green chili, slit lengthwise
- 100 gm. / 3.5 oz. green beans, sliced into 1-inch pieces
- 1 small-medium carrot, chopped
- 1 small-medium zucchini, chopped
- 1 small eggplant, cubed (optional)
- 2 medium tomatoes, chopped
- 1/4 teaspoon salt (adjust to taste)
- 3 cups water
- 1 teaspoon jaggery powder (or sugar)

To prepare tadka,

- 1 tablespoon oil
- 1/2 teaspoon mustard seeds
- Pinch of asafoetida
- 2 whole dried red chilies
- 8-10 fresh/dried curry leaves

Instructions

Step A : Soak the lentil

1. Soak dal in 1 cup of water for 30 min.

Step B : Prepare tamarind water

2. In a small bowl, add tamarind paste + 1/4 cup warm water. Stir and dissolve. Set aside.

3. Set a pan over medium heat. Add oil. Once it's hot, add cumin seeds + coriander seeds + fenugreek seeds + chana dal. Stir and sauté for 1 min. Now add asafoetida + cloves + green cardamom + onion + ginger + garlic + red chilies. Stir-sauté for 3-4 min, or until the onion is golden.

4. Add turmeric powder + Kashmiri red chili powder + salt. Turn down the heat to low-medium and stir-sauté for 2-3 min (stirring continuously).

5. Turn off the heat and allow the mixture to cool down a bit. Once it's cool, transfer the masala to a blender/grinder. Add 1/4 cup water and blend to a smooth paste (this is the sambar masala). Set aside.

Step D : Prepare sambar

6. Set your electric / stovetop / jiggle-top pressure cooker to medium heat. Add oil. Once it's hot, add green chili + green beans + carrot + zucchini + eggplant + tomatoes + salt. Stir and sauté for 2 min, or until the veggies soften a bit.

7. Now add the sambar masala + soaked (and drained) toor dal + 3 cups of water.

8. For electric pressure cooker - Secure the lid, seal the knob, press MANUAL (or PRESSURE COOK) & set the timer to 10 MINUTES on HIGH PRESSURE. Let the pressure release naturally for 8-10 minutes.

   For stovetop pressure cooker - Secure the lid, seal the valve, turn the heat up to high and when the cooker indicates it has reached high pressure, lower the heat to maintain it and begin counting 10 min pressure cooking time. Turn off the heat and allow the pressure to release naturally for 8-10 minutes.

   For jiggle-top pressure cooker - Secure the lid, put the whistle on, and cook over medium heat for 4-5 whistles. Let the pressure release naturally for 8-10 minutes.

9. Open the lid and stir in the tamarind water + jaggery powder (or sugar). Bring the mixture to a gentle simmer.

Step E : Prepare tadka

10. Set a sauté pan (or tadka pan) over medium heat. Add oil.

11. Once it's hot, add mustard seeds + asafoetida + dried red chilies + curry leaves and let the seeds splutter.

12. As the chilies start to turn dark, immediately pour the tadka over the sambar. Give it a stir. Adjust salt and serve with dosa, idli, or rice!

Aloo Matar

Potato + peas are cooked in a tomato-based gravy.

Prep - 7 min.   Cook - 25 min.   Servings - 2 to 3

Ingredients

- 2 tablespoons neutral oil
- 1 teaspoon cumin seeds
- 4 garlic cloves, chopped
- 1-inch ginger, chopped
- 1 onion, chopped
- 2 potatoes, chopped
- 3 tomatoes, chopped
- 1/2 teaspoon turmeric powder
- 1/2 teaspoon coriander powder
- 1/2 teaspoon cumin powder
- 1/2 teaspoon Kashmiri chili powder
- 1/2 teaspoon salt (adjust to taste)
- 1 cup peas (fresh or frozen)
- 1.5 cups water
- 1/4 cup freshly chopped cilantro

Instructions

1. Set a sauté pan over medium heat. Add oil. Once it's hot, add cumin seeds. Let it splutter for 30-40 seconds.

2. Add garlic + ginger + onion. Stir- sauté for 3-4 minutes, or until the onion is golden.

3. Next, add potatoes and stir-sauté for 5 minutes. Then add tomatoes + turmeric powder + coriander powder + cumin powder + Kashmiri red chili powder + salt.

4. Stir and cook for 4-5 minutes, or until the tomatoes get mushy.

5. Add peas + water. Mix well, cover the pan, and cook for 10 min over low-medium heat.

6. Remove the pan from heat. Sprinkle freshly chopped cilantro. Enjoy!

Jeera Aloo

Boiled potatoes are fried with cumin seeds (Jeera) + spices.

Prep - 5 min.   Cook - 25 min.   Servings - 2 to 3

Ingredients

- 500 gm. (18 oz.) potatoes
- 2 tablespoons neutral oil
- 1 teaspoon cumin seeds
- 1 onion, sliced
- Pinch of asafoetida
- 1/4 teaspoon turmeric powder
- 1/4 teaspoon Kashmiri red chili powder
- 1/2 teaspoon coriander powder
- Salt
- 1 teaspoon amchur
  (dried mango powder)
- 2 tablespoons water
- 1/4 cup freshly chopped cilantro

Instructions

1. Rinse, peel, and cut the potatoes into bite-sized (around 1 inch) chunks.
   Boil until they're tender (don't overcook or they won't hold their shape).

2. Once boiled, drain and set aside.

3. Set a pan over medium heat. Add oil. Once it's hot, add cumin seeds and let it splutter for 30-40 sec.

4. Add onion + asafoetida. Stir and sauté for 2 minutes, or until the onions get translucent.

5. Add turmeric powder + Kashmiri red chili powder + coriander powder + salt + amchur + water. Stir and cook for 1-2 min.

6. Add the boiled potatoes and mix and fold gently with the spices.
   Cook for 1 minute.

7. Turn off the heat. Sprinkle freshly chopped cilantro and mix some more.

Soy Chunks Curry

Soy Chunks (TVP) are cooked with masala gravy.

Prep - 5 min.   Cook - 35 min.   Servings - 2 to 3

Ingredients

To boil soy chunks,

- 2 cups soy chunks (TVP, or soy curls)
- 1 teaspoon salt
- 2 cups water

To marinate & fry soy chunks,

- 1 tablespoon oil
- 1 tablespoon ginger-garlic paste
- 1/2 tsp Kashmiri red chili powder
- To prepare tomato-cashew paste,
- 1 tablespoon oil
- 1-inch ginger, sliced
- 5 garlic cloves, halved
- 2 onions, roughly sliced
- 1/4 cup cashews
- 3 tomatoes, roughly chopped

To prepare masala gravy,

- 1 tablespoon oil
- 2 bay leaves
- 3 green cardamoms
- 1/2 teaspoon cumin seeds
- 1/4 teaspoon turmeric powder
- 1/2 teaspoon coriander powder
- 1/2 teaspoon cumin powder
- 1/2 tsp Kashmiri red chili powder
- 1 cup water
- Salt, to taste
- 1/2 teaspoon garam masala
- 1/4 cup freshly chopped cilantro

Instructions

Step A : Boil, marinate, fry soy chunks

1. Heat 2 cups of water in a saucepan. Add the soy chunks + salt and boil for 1-2 minutes.

2. Drain the boiled chunks into a large sieve and let it cool for 5-6 minutes. Once cooled, squeeze the soy chunks and remove excess water. Then transfer them to a mixing bowl.

3. To the bowl, add ginger-garlic paste + Kashmiri chili powder. Mix well and let it marinade for 5 min.

4. Set a sauté pan over medium heat. Add oil. Once it's hot, add marinated soy chunks and sauté for 5-6 minutes.

Step B : Prepare the tomato-cashew paste

5. Rinse the pan and set it over medium heat. Add oil. Once it's hot, add ginger + garlic + onion. Stir-sauté for 3-4 min, or until the onion is golden. Add cashews + tomato and stir-cook for 4-5 minutes, or until the tomato softens.

6. Turn off the heat. Transfer everything to a bowl and let them cool for 5 min. Then blend to a fine paste. Set aside.

Step C : Prepare the tomato gravy

7. Rinse the pan and set it over medium heat. Add oil.

8. Once it's hot, add bay leaves + cardamoms + cumin seeds. Sauté for 30-40 sec, or until the cumin seeds splutter and turn brown.

9. Add the blended tomato-cashew paste + turmeric powder + coriander powder + cumin powder + Kashmiri red chili powder + salt.

10. Mix well, cover the pan, turn down the heat to low, and cook for 8-10 minutes. Stir occasionally.

11. Next, add the soy chunks + water + garam masala. Mix well, cover the pan, and cook for 7-8 min over low heat.

12. Turn off the heat, discard bay leaves, and stir in freshly chopped cilantro. Soy chunks curry is ready. Serve with rice or flatbread of your choice.

Pumpkin Chana Sabji

Brown chickpeas are cooked w/pumpkin & spices.

Prep - 10 min.   Cook - 22 min.   Servings - 2 to 3

Ingredients

- 1 cup kala chana (brown chickpeas)
- 1 tablespoon coconut oil
- 4 cloves garlic, chopped
- 1-inch piece ginger, chopped
- 1 onion, chopped
- 14 oz. (400 gm.) pumpkin - peeled, seeds and strings removed, and cut into bite-size chunks
- 1/2 teaspoon turmeric powder
- 1/2 teaspoon cumin powder
- 1/2 teaspoon coriander powder
- 1/2 tsp Kashmiri red chili powder
- 1 teaspoon salt (adjust to taste)
- 3 tomatoes, chopped
- 1.5 cups water
- 1 onion, freshly chopped (to garnish)
- 1/4 cup freshly chopped cilantro (to garnish)

Instructions

1. Rinse, drain, and transfer kala chana to a large bowl. Add 4 cups water & soak overnight.

2. *Next day* Set your pressure cooker over medium heat. Add oil.

3. Once it's hot, add garlic + ginger + onion. Stir-sauté for 3-4 min, or until the onion is golden.

4. Add the soaked and drained kala chana. Stir and mix well. Cover the cooker (do not seal), and cook for 5 min, stirring occasionally.

5. Add pumpkin + turmeric powder + cumin powder + coriander powder + Kashmiri red chili powder + salt + tomatoes. Stir and mix.

6. Cover the cooker (do not seal), and cook for 3-4 min, stirring occasionally.

7. Add water and give it a quick stir.

8. For electric pressure cooker - Secure the lid, seal the knob, press MANUAL (or PRESSURE COOK) and set the timer to 10 min on HIGH PRESSURE. Let the pressure release naturally for 8-10 minutes.

    For stovetop pressure cooker - Secure the lid, seal the pressure valve, turn the heat to high and when the cooker indicates it has reached high pressure, lower the heat to maintain it and begin counting 10 min pressure cooking time. Turn off the heat and allow the pressure to release naturally for 8-10 minutes.

    For jiggle-top pressure cooker - Secure the lid, put the whistle on, and cook over medium heat for 5-6 whistles. Let the pressure release naturally for 8-10 minutes.

9. Open the lid and mash the pumpkin using a potato masher. Add freshly chopped onion + cilantro. Stir well.

10. Pumpkin chana sabji is ready. Serve over rice, roti, or your fav flatbreads.

Matar Mushroom Masala

Peas & mushrooms are cooked in spiced tomato gravy.

Prep - 7 min.   Cook - 25 min.   Servings - 3

Ingredients

To prepare tomato-cashew paste,

- 1 tablespoon oil
- 1 large onion, sliced
- 2 green chilies, chopped
- 1-inch ginger, sliced
- 4 garlic cloves, sliced
- 4 medium tomatoes, roughly chopped
- 1/4 cup cashews (soaked for 30 minutes)

To prepare gravy,

- 1 tablespoon oil
- 1/2 teaspoon cumin seeds
- 1 bay leaf
- 1/4 teaspoon turmeric powder
- 1 teaspoon coriander powder
- 1/2 teaspoon cumin powder
- 1/2 tsp Kashmiri red chili powder
- 1/2 teaspoon salt (adjust to taste)
- 9 oz./250 gm. green peas (fresh or frozen)
- 9 oz./250 gm. button mushrooms, sliced
- 1/2 teaspoon garam masala
- 1 cup water chopped
- 1/4 cup freshly chopped cilantro
- 1/2 teaspoon kasuri methi (dried fenugreek leaves)

Step A : Prepare tomato-cashew paste

1. Set a pan over medium heat. Add oil. Once it's hot, add onion + green chilies + ginger + garlic. Stir-sauté for 3-4 min, or until the onion is golden.

2. Add tomatoes + soaked (and drained) cashews and stir-cook for 4-5 minutes, or until the tomato softens.

3. Turn off the heat. Transfer everything to a bowl & let them cool for 5-6 min. Then blend to a fine paste. Set aside.

Step B : Prepare gravy

4. Rinse the pan and set it over medium heat. Add oil.

5. Once it's hot, add cumin seeds + bay leaf and sauté for 30-40 seconds, or until the cumin seeds splutter.

6. Add the blended tomato-cashew paste + turmeric powder + coriander powder + cumin powder + Kashmiri red chili powder + salt to the pan.

7. Mix well, cover the pan, reduce the heat to low, and cook for 8-10 minutes.

8. Once the mixture is cooked and turns thick & red, add green peas + mushrooms + garam masala powder + water. Stir and cook for 5-6 minutes.

9. Turn off the heat. Garnish with freshly chopped cilantro + dried fenugreek leaves and serve with naan, or rice.

Baingan Bharta

Eggplant (Baingan) is charred, mashed & cooked w/spices.

Prep - 7 min.   Cook - 25 min.   Servings - 3

Ingredients

- 2 large eggplants
- 4 garlic cloves, whole
- 2 green chilies, whole
- 1.5 tablespoons oil
- 1/2 teaspoon cumin seeds
- Pinch of asafoetida
- 1 large onion, chopped
- 1-inch ginger, finely chopped
- 4 garlic cloves, finely chopped
- 1/4 teaspoon turmeric powder
- 1 tsp Kashmiri red chili powder
- 1/2 teaspoon cumin powder
- 1/2 teaspoon coriander powder
- 4 medium tomatoes, chopped
- 1/2 teaspoon salt (adjust to taste)
- 1/4 cup freshly chopped cilantro
- 1/2 tsp garam masala powder

Instructions

Step A : Make slits

1. Using a sharp knife, make four vertical slits in each eggplant. The slits should not go all the way through the eggplant, so it remains intact while roasting.

2. Stuff whole garlic cloves (peeled) + whole green chilies in the slits of each eggplant.

Step B : Roast the eggplants

3. Transfer the eggplants to an open flame stovetop / grill and roast them over medium-high heat for 10-12 min, or until the skin is completely charred, and the eggplants turn soft and pulpy. Make sure you turn them every 2 min so they're roasted evenly.
Note: You can either roast them on open flame (stovetop), or on a grill, or in an

oven. Roasting in an oven won't give Bharta that authentic smoky flavor.

Step C : Remove the skin

4. Once roasted, let the eggplants cool for 10-15 min. Then peel and remove the skin. Mash everything (eggplants + garlic cloves + green chilies) using a potato masher and set aside.

Step D : Prepare the masala

5. Set a pan over medium heat. Add oil. Once it's hot, add cumin seeds and let it splutter for 30-40 seconds.

6. Add asafoetida + onion. Stir-sauté for 2-3 min, or until the onion is translucent.

7. Add ginger + garlic, and stir-cook for 1 minute. Next, add tomatoes + turmeric powder + Kashmiri red chili powder + cumin powder + coriander powder + salt. Stir and cook for 5-6 min, or until the tomatoes get mushy.

8. Now, add the mashed eggplant + garam masala powder. Mix well, turn down the heat to low and cook for 2 minutes.

9. Turn off the heat and sprinkle freshly chopped cilantro. Mix well.

10. Baingan Bharta is ready! Enjoy with roti, bread, or rice.

Aloo Gobi   Classic potato-cauliflower curry.

Prep - 10 min.   Cook - 25 min.   Servings - 3

Ingredients

- 2 tablespoons coconut oil
- 1 teaspoon cumin seeds
- 4 garlic cloves, finely chopped
- 1-inch ginger, finely chopped
- 1 onion, chopped
- Pinch of asafoetida
- 2 medium potatoes, chopped
- 4 cups cauliflower florets
- 1/4 teaspoon turmeric powder
- 1/2 teaspoon cumin powder
- 1/2 teaspoon coriander powder
- 1/2 tsp Kashmiri red chili powder
- 1/2 teaspoon salt (adjust to taste)
- 2 tomatoes, chopped
- 1/2 cup green peas, fresh/frozen
- Handful of chopped cilantro

Instructions

1. Set a pan over medium heat. Add oil. Once it's hot, add cumin seeds. Let it splutter for 30-40 seconds. Then add garlic + ginger + onion + asafoetida & stir-sauté for 3-4 min, or until the onion is golden.

2. Add potatoes and give them a quick mix. Cover the pan and sauté for 5 minutes (stir occasionally). Next, add cauliflower florets. Stir well, cover the pan, and cook for 3-4 minutes.

3. Next, add turmeric powder + cumin powder + coriander powder + Kashmiri red chili powder + salt. Stir and cook for 1 minute.

4. Add tomatoes + green peas. Mix well, cover the pan, and cook for 9-10 min. Stir occasionally. Garnish with freshly chopped cilantro and serve.

Shimla Mirch Curry

Spicy & aromatic combo of bell peppers & potatoes.

Prep - 5 min.   Cook - 20 min.   Servings - 3

Ingredients

- 2 tablespoons oil
- 1 teaspoon cumin seeds
- 1 medium onion, chopped
- Pinch of asafoetida
- 2 medium potatoes, cut into bite-size pieces
- 4 garlic cloves, grated
- 1-inch ginger, grated
- 1/4 teaspoon turmeric powder
- 1/2 tsp Kashmiri red chili powder
- 1 teaspoon coriander powder
- 2 large tomatoes, chopped
- 1/2 teaspoon salt (adjust to taste)
- 3 green bell peppers, cut into bite-size pieces
- 1/2 teaspoon garam masala
- 1/4 cup freshly chopped cilantro

Instructions

1. Set a pan over medium heat. Add oil. Once it's hot, add cumin seeds. Let them splutter for 30-40 sec. Then add onion + asafoetida and sauté for 2-3 min, or until the onion is golden.

2. Add potatoes and stir-sauté for 2 min. Cover the pan and cook for 4-5 min, or until the potatoes start to soften.

3. Add ginger + garlic and stir-cook for 1 minute. Next, add turmeric powder + Kashmiri red chili powder + coriander powder. Stir well and cook for 1 min.

4. Add tomatoes + salt and give it a good stir. Cover the pan and cook for 4-5 min, or until the tomatoes are mushy.

5. Next, add the bell peppers + garam masala. Mix well, cover the pan, and cook for 3-5 min, over medium heat. Turn off the heat and garnish with freshly chopped cilantro.

Aloo Bhindi

Do you dislike okra because it's slimy? Try this recipe.

Prep - 10 min.   Cook - 20 min.   Servings - 2

Ingredients

- 2 tablespoons oil
- 1/2 teaspoon paanch furan (recipe on Page 104)
- 3 garlic cloves, chopped
- Pinch of asafoetida
- 1 green chili, chopped
- 2 medium potatoes, chopped
- 1/4 teaspoon turmeric powder
- 1/2 tsp Kashmiri red chili powder
- 1/2 teaspoon coriander powder
- 1/2 teaspoon cumin powder
- 18 oz. (500 gm.) okra, cut into bite-size pieces
- 1 large onion, cut into petals
- 1/2 teaspoon salt (adjust to taste)
- 1 teaspoon dried mango powder

Instructions

1. Set a pan over medium heat. Add oil. Once it's hot, add paanch furan and sauté for 30-40 sec, or until aromatic.

2. Add garlic + asafoetida + green chili. Stir-sauté for 1 minute.

3. Next, add potatoes and stir-cook for 5-6 min, or until they soften up a bit (cover the pan as you're cooking them).

4. Add turmeric powder + Kashmiri red chili powder + coriander powder + cumin powder. Mix well and cook for 2 minutes.

5. Now add okra and stir-sauté for 5 min (do not cover the pan).

6. Add onion + salt + dried mango powder. Mix well, and cook for 5 minutes (stir frequently, do not cover the pan). Aloo Bhindi is ready. Serve warm with rice or roti. Enjoy!

Broccoli Curry

Rich, quick & easy broccoli potato curry.

Prep - 10 min.   Cook - 22 min.   Servings - 2

Ingredients

- 2 onions, roughly chopped
- 1-inch piece ginger
- 2 garlic cloves
- 2 green chilies
- 2 tomatoes, quartered
- 1 tablespoon coconut oil
- 1/2 teaspoon cumin seeds
- 1/4 teaspoon turmeric powder
- 1/2 teaspoon cumin powder
- 1/2 teaspoon coriander powder
- Salt (adjust to taste)
- 2 cups broccoli florets (steamed)
- 1 medium potato
  (cut into bite-size pieces and steamed)
- 3/4 cup water
- 1/2 cup coconut cream
- Handful of chopped cilantro

Instructions

1. In a blender (or a food processor), add onion + ginger + garlic + green chilies + tomatoes. Blend and set aside.

2. Set a pan over low-medium heat. Add coconut oil. Once it's hot, add cumin seeds and let them splutter for 30-40 seconds.

3. Add the tomato mixture + turmeric powder + cumin powder + coriander powder + salt. Mix well and cook for 10-12 min (over medium heat), or until the mixture turns thick and paste-like. Stir frequently to avoid burning.

4. Add steamed broccoli + potatoes + 3/4 cup water. Stir and mix. Cover with the lid and cook for 6-8 minutes over low-medium heat.

5. Stir in the coconut cream. Garnish with freshly chopped cilantro.

6. Broccoli curry is ready. Serve with rice, naans, rotis, or your fav flatbreads.

Malai Kofta

Potato-tofu 'dumplings' (Kofta) served w/creamy gravy (Malai).

Prep - 12 min.   Cook - 28 min.   Makes - 12 kofta

Ingredients

To prepare the Malai,

- 1.5 tablespoons coconut oil
- 1/2 teaspoon cumin seeds
- 1 cinnamon stick
- 1 bay leaf
- 3 cloves
- 1 black cardamom
- 3 green cardamoms
- 1 large onion, chopped
- 1 green chili, chopped
- 4 garlic cloves, chopped
- 1-inch ginger, chopped
- 1/4 teaspoon turmeric powder
- 1 tsp Kashmiri red chili powder
- 1 teaspoon coriander powder
- 1/2 teaspoon cumin powder
- 4 medium tomatoes, chopped
- 1/2 cup cashews
- 1/2 teaspoon salt (adjust to taste)
- 2 cups water
- 1/2 tsp dried fenugreek leaves
- 1 tablespoon sugar
- 1/4 cup coconut cream
- Handful of chopped cilantro

To prepare the Kofta,

- 9 oz. / 250 gm. tofu, crumbled
- 9 oz. / 250 gm. potato, boiled & mashed

- Handful of chopped cilantro
- 1 tablespoon minced ginger
- 1 green chili, chopped
- 1.5 tablespoons cornstarch (add more if required)
- 1/2 teaspoon salt
- 2 tablespoons finely chopped cashews
- Oil, for deep frying

Instructions

Step A : Prepare the gravy

1. Set a pan over medium heat. Add oil. Once it's hot, add cumin seeds + cinnamon + bay leaf + cloves + black cardamom + green cardamoms.
Stir-sauté for 1 minute.

2. Next, add onions + green chili & sauté for 3-4 minutes, or until the onions start to turn golden. Then add garlic + ginger. Stir & cook for 2 minutes.

3. Now, add the spices (turmeric powder + red chili powder + coriander powder + cumin powder).

4. Stir and sauté for 1 minute. Then add tomatoes + cashews + salt. Stir and cook for 5-6 minutes, or until the tomatoes are wilted.

5. Add water and give it a quick stir. Cover the pan and cook over low-medium heat for 5 minutes.

6. Turn off the heat. Open the lid, and let it cool for 8-10 min. In the meantime, let's prep the dumpling.

Step B : Prepare and deep-fry the Kofta

7. In a large bowl, add crumbled tofu + mashed potatoes + cilantro + ginger + green chili + cornstarch + salt + cashews. Mix well using your hands. Scoop around 1.5 tablespoons of the mixture and roll it into a ball. Repeat the same for the remaining mixture.

8. Set a pan over medium heat. Add oil (to deep fry). Once it's hot, add the dumplings and deep-fry until golden brown. Place them over a paper towel and set aside.

Step C : Blend the gravy and pour it over the Kofta

9. Transfer the (cooled) gravy to a blender and blend it to a fine puree. Pour it into a pan. For a silky texture, strain the puree with a sieve.

10. Set the pan over low-medium heat. Add fenugreek leaves + sugar. Adjust salt and stir. Once it starts to simmer, turn off the heat and add coconut cream. Give it a quick stir.

11. Pour it over the dumplings, and sprinkle freshly chopped cilantro on top. Malai Kofta is ready. Serve hot.

Vegan Butter Chicken

Iconic butter chicken, but vegan! Made with seitan.

Prep - 11 min.   Cook - 35 min.   Servings - 3 to 4

Ingredients

To prepare seitan,

- 1/2 cup vital wheat gluten
- 2 tablespoons nutritional yeast
- 1/2 teaspoon garlic powder
- 1/2 teaspoon onion powder
- 1/2 teaspoon smoked paprika
- Salt & pepper
- 1 teaspoon vegan BBQ seasoning mix (optional)
- 1 teaspoon soy sauce
- 1/2 cup warm water
- 4 cups veggie stock (or water)
- 1 tablespoon oil

To prepare gravy,

- 2 tablespoons vegan butter (or oil)
- 1 bay leaf
- 1 stick cinnamon
- 4 cloves
- 3 green cardamoms
- 4 garlic cloves, chopped
- 1-inch ginger, chopped
- 2 onions, sliced
- 1/2 cup tomato puree
- 1/4 teaspoon turmeric powder
- 1/2 teaspoon coriander powder
- 1/2 teaspoon cumin powder
- 1/2 teaspoon salt (adjust to taste)
- 1 cup water
- 1/4 cup coconut cream
- 1/4 cup freshly chopped cilantro

Step A : Prepare the seitan pieces

1. In a large mixing bowl, add vital wheat gluten + nutritional yeast + garlic powder + onion powder + smoked paprika + salt + pepper + BBQ mix.

2. Stir and mix well. Then add soy sauce + warm water. Using a spatula, combine the dry + wet ingredients. As it starts to form a dough, switch over to your hands and knead well.

   Note: Kneading is really important (I knead the dough for 7-10 minutes). A well-kneaded seitan is 'meaty' and elastic.

3. Tear the seitan into smaller chunks (around 1-inch pieces) and set aside.

4. Heat a saucepan and add 4 cups veggie broth. Bring it to a simmer. Now add the seitan chunks and gently simmer for 8-10 minutes. Turn off the heat. Remove and drain the pieces.

5. Set a pan over medium heat. Add 1 tablespoon oil. Once it's hot, add the seitan pieces and sauté for 4-5 min, or until it starts to brown. Transfer to a bowl and set aside.

Step B : Prepare the gravy

6. Set the same pan over medium heat. Add 2 tablespoons vegan butter (or oil). Once it's hot, add bay leaf + cinnamon stick + cloves + cardamoms.

7. Stir and sauté for 1 minute, or until fragrant. Add garlic + ginger + onion.

8. Stir- sauté for 3-4 minutes, or until the onions turn golden brown.

9. Add tomato puree + turmeric + coriander + cumin + salt. Mix well, put the lid on, and cook for 8-10 min over low heat (stir occasionally).

10. Open the lid, add 1 cup water and mix well. Add the browned seitan pieces and mix some more.

11. Cover with the lid and cook for 5 min over low-medium heat.

12. Turn off the heat. Add coconut cream + freshly chopped cilantro & give it a gentle stir. Vegan butter chicken is ready. Serve over rice, roti, or naan.

Kadai Tofu

Tofu cubes are fried in spiced tomato-onion gravy.

Prep - 10 min.   Cook - 30 min.   Servings - 2

Ingredients

To prepare kadai masala,

- 1 teaspoon coriander seeds
- 1 teaspoon cumin seeds
- 1/2 teaspoon fennel seeds
- 1/2 teaspoon black peppercorns
- 4 cloves
- 2 green cardamoms
- 2 whole dried red chilies

To sauté tofu,

- 10 oz. (300 gm.) firm tofu, cut into bite-size cubes
- 1 tablespoon oil
- Pinch of salt

To sauté veggies,

- 1/2 tablespoon oil
- 2 bell peppers, cut into bite-size pieces
- 1 large onion, cut into petals

To prepare gravy,

- 2 tablespoons oil
- 1 bay leaf
- 4 garlic cloves, chopped
- 1-inch ginger, chopped
- 2 medium onions, chopped
- 3-4 medium tomatoes, chopped
- 1/4 teaspoon turmeric powder
- 1/2 tsp Kashmiri red chili powder
- 1/2 teaspoon salt (adjust to taste)
- 1/2 cup water
- 1/2 tsp dried fenugreek leaves
- 1/4 cup freshly chopped cilantro

Instructions

Step A : Prepare the kadai masala *

1. Set a pan over low heat. Add all the Kadai Masala ingredients. Stir and roast for 2-3 min, or until fragrant. Transfer to a blender (or a spice grinder) and blend in short bursts until finely coarse. Set aside.

Step B : Sauté tofu

2. Set the pan over medium heat. Add oil. Once it's hot, add tofu and sauté on all sides until golden and crispy. Transfer to a large bowl.

3. Sprinkle 1 tablespoon kadai masala + a pinch of salt over the tofu. Toss & coat.

Step C : Sauté veggies

4. Add 1/2 tablespoon oil to the pan. Once it's hot, add onion + bell pepper. Stir-sauté for 2-3 min, or until they're soft. Set aside in a bowl.

Step D : Prepare the gravy

5. Rinse, clean, and dry the pan (or use a separate pan). Set it over medium heat and add 1 tablespoon oil. Once it's hot, add bay leaf + garlic + ginger + onion. Stir-sauté for 3-4 min, or until the onion is golden.

6. Next, add the tomatoes and stir-cook for 4-5 minutes, or until they're soft.

7. Turn off the heat and let it cool for 5-10 minutes. Once cooled, remove the bay leaf, transfer the mixture to a blender, and blend until smooth.

8. Rinse, clean, and dry the pan (or use a separate pan). Set it over medium heat and add 1 tablespoon oil. Once it's hot, add the blended gravy + remaining kadai masala + turmeric powder + Kashmiri red chili powder + salt.

9. Stir-cook for 10-12 minutes, or until the oil starts to separate at the edge of the pan.

10. Add water + sautéed onion + bell peppers + tofu. Stir and mix. Cover the pan and let it simmer for 2-3 minutes.

11. Uncover the pan, and sprinkle dried fenugreek leaves + cilantro.
    Kadai tofu is ready! Enjoy with rice or breads.

***Note**

You can also make a large portion of kadai masala and store it in an airtight container. It will remain fresh for 2-3 weeks.

Palak Tofu

Spinach is cooked with tomato mixture, then fried w/tofu.

Prep - 8 min.   Cook - 25 min.   Servings - 2

Ingredients

- 2 tablespoons oil
- 1/2 teaspoon cumin seeds
- 1 onion, chopped
- 4 garlic cloves, chopped
- 1/2 inch ginger, chopped
- 1 green chili, slit lengthwise
- 2 medium tomatoes, chopped
- 1/2 cup cashews, soaked for 20 min.
- 1/2 teaspoon salt (adjust to taste)
- 9 oz. (250 gm.) spinach
- 9 oz. (250 gm.) firm tofu, cubed
- 1/4 teaspoon turmeric powder
- 1/2 teaspoon coriander powder
- 1/2 teaspoon cumin powder
- 1/4 cup water
- 1/4 cup coconut cream (or milk)
- 1/4 teaspoon garam masala

Instructions

Step A : Cook and blend the spinach

1. Set a pan over low-medium heat. Add 1 tablespoon oil.

2. Once it's hot, add cumin seeds. Let it splutter for 30-40 seconds.

3. Add onion + garlic + ginger + green chili and sauté for 3-4 minutes over medium heat, or until the onion turns golden.

4. Add tomatoes + soaked cashews + salt. Stir and cook for 4-5 minutes.

5. Add spinach. Stir and cook until wilted, about 2-3 minutes.

6. Turn off the heat and let it cool for a while. Then transfer everything to a blender and blend until creamy.

7. Next, add 1 tablespoon oil to the pan. Once it's hot, add the cubed tofu. Stir & sauté for 3 min. Then add turmeric + cumin + coriander powder.

8. Sauté for 4-5 min over low heat on all sides. Make sure the spices don't burn.

Step C : Mix spinach puree & tofu

9. Add water and gently scrape the bottom of the pan to remove any brown bits. Stir and cook for 1 min.

10. Next, add spinach puree. Stir and cook for 1-2 minutes over low heat.

11. Turn off the heat. Add coconut cream + garam masala, and give it a quick stir. Serve with rice or your fav breads.

Tofu Tikka Masala

Restaurant-style grilled tofu.

Prep - 10 min.   Cook - 22 min.   Servings - 2

Ingredients

Masala Ingredients

- 1/3 cup (80 ml.) soy yogurt, or coconut yogurt
- 1 teaspoon roasted cumin powder
- 1/2 tsp roasted coriander powder
- 1/2 teaspoon garam masala
- 1/2 teaspoon red chili powder
- 1/2 tsp Kashmiri red chili powder
- 1/4 teaspoon turmeric powder
- 1/4 teaspoon ground nutmeg
- 2 tablespoons besan (Bengal gram flour)
- 1 teaspoon dried fenugreek leaves
- 1 tablespoon lemon juice
- 1 tablespoon ginger-garlic paste
- 1/2 teaspoon salt (adjust to taste)
- 1/4 teaspoon pepper
- 2 tablespoons oil

Tikka Ingredients

- 7 oz. (200 gm.) firm tofu, cut into bite-size cubes
- 2 bell peppers, cut into 1-inch petals
- 2 onions, cut into 1-inch petals

Instructions

1. In a large mixing bowl, combine all the masala ingredients, except oil.

2. Heat oil on a pan. Once it's hot, pour it over the mixture in the bowl. Stir and mix well using a spatula.

3. Transfer tofu + bell peppers + onions to the large bowl and mix well with the masala. Set aside for at least 20 min.

4. After 20 min: You can prepare the tikka masala by frying them on a pan, or over a grill (using skewers), or over a direct flame.

5. To prepare on a pan: Heat a pan over medium-high heat. Once it's hot, place the tofu + bell peppers + onions all over the pan and sauté on all sides (use tongs) until the edges of the tofu is lightly browned and the bell peppers and onions are slightly charred. Do not stir.

   To prepare over a grill or a flame: Thread the tofu, bell peppers, and onion onto your skewers. Once the grill is hot, grill the skewers on all sides for 5-6 minutes, or until the edges of tofu and veggies are lightly charred.

   Alternatively, you can also cook over stove top flame which takes 2-3 min.

6. Tofu Tikka Masala is ready. Garnish with freshly chopped cilantro.
   Serve with rice, naan, or your choice of side.

Golden Tofu Curry

Tofu + veggie curry, enriched by coconut milk.

Prep - 12 min. Cook - 38 min. Servings - 2 to 3

Ingredients

- 1 tablespoon oil
- 3 garlic cloves, chopped
- 1-inch ginger, chopped
- 1 onion, chopped
- 1 cup tomato puree
- 1/4 teaspoon turmeric powder
- 1/2 teaspoon cumin powder
- 1/2 teaspoon coriander powder
- 1/2 tsp Kashmiri red chili powder
- 1/2 tsp salt (adjust to taste)
- 1/4 tsp black pepper powder
- 1/2 cup carrot, chopped
- 1 cup green peas (fresh or frozen)
- 1 cup cauliflower florets
- 1 medium potato, chopped
- 1 tbsp jaggery powder (or sugar)
- 1 cup water
- 8.8 oz. (250 gm.) firm tofu, cubed
- 2 cups coconut milk
- 1 teaspoon garam masala
- Freshly chopped cilantro

Instructions

1. Set a large pan over medium heat. Add oil. Once it's hot, add garlic + ginger + onion and stir-sauté for 3-4 minutes, or until the onion's golden.

2. Add tomato puree + turmeric powder + cumin powder + coriander powder + Kashmiri red chili powder + salt + pepper. Mix well, cover the pan, and cook for 3-4 min (stir occasionally).

3. Next, add carrots + green peas + cauliflower florets + potatoes + jaggery powder + water. Mix well. Cover the pan and simmer for 15 minutes.

4. Uncover the pan and add tofu + coconut milk. Stir gently. Cover the pan and simmer for 15 more minutes.

5. Turn off the heat and sprinkle garam masala + freshly chopped cilantro. Give everything a gentle mix. Serve hot over rice.

Aloo Tikki   Potatoes are boiled, mashed, mixed w/spices, then fried.

Prep - 10 min.   Cook - 12 min.   Servings - 2 to 3

Ingredients

- 18 oz. (500 gm.) potatoes - boiled, peeled, and cooled
- Pinch of asafoetida
- 1/2 teaspoon cumin seeds
- 1-inch ginger, chopped
- 1 green chili, chopped
- 1/4 teaspoon turmeric powder
- 1/2 tsp Kashmiri red chili powder
- 1/2 teaspoon coriander powder
- 1/2 teaspoon dried mango powder
- 1/2 teaspoon garam masala
- 1/2 teaspoon salt (adjust to taste)
- 1/4 teaspoon black salt
- 1/4 cup freshly chopped cilantro
- 2 tablespoons cornstarch (or rice flour)
- 3 tablespoons oil (more if needed)

Instructions

Step A : Prepare the patty

1. Add all the patty ingredients (everything except oil) to a large mixing bowl.

2. Mix and mash until they're well combined. Scoop around 1/4 cup of this mixture and using your palms, turn it into a patty-like shape. Transfer it to a plate. Repeat the same for the remaining mixture. Chill them for 2 hours.

Step B : Fry

3. Set a non-stick pan over medium heat. Add 1 tablespoon oil. Once it's hot, add the chilled patties (in batches) and fry for 2-3 min on each side, or until they're brown on both sides.

4. Fry the remaining batches using the remaining oil (add more if needed).
   Aloo tikki is ready. Enjoy with green chutney and imli chutney.

Pyaaz Pakoda

Thinly sliced onion is mixed with spices, then deep-fried.

Prep - 2 min.   Cook - 11 min.   Makes - 15 pakodas

Ingredients

- 1 large potato, peeled and grated
- 2 large onions, thinly sliced
- 3 tablespoons besan (Bengal gram flour)
- 2 tablespoons rice flour
- 1 tablespoon minced garlic
- 1/2 tablespoon minced ginger
- 1 green chili, chopped
- 1/2 teaspoon turmeric powder
- 1 teaspoon roasted cumin powder
- Salt, to taste
- 1/4 cup freshly chopped cilantro
- Oil, to deep fry

Instructions

1. Mix all the ingredients (except oil) in a large mixing bowl. Lightly squeeze the mixture so as to release the juices from onions & potatoes. Mix some more and set aside.

2. Set a deep, frying pan over high heat. Add oil (make sure the level of oil is at least 2-inches from the bottom of the pan).

3. Once it's hot, turn down the heat to medium. Scoop around 2 tablespoons of the mixture and gently drop it into the pan.

   NOTE: You can make around 4-6 pakodas at a time, but this depends upon the size of your pan. Make sure the pakodas don't touch each other.

4. Deep fry for 2 min, or until golden and crispy. Remove the pakodas and place them on a paper towel. Repeat the same for the remaining batches.
   Dip pakodas in Ketchup or Imli chutney and serve hot.

Gobi Pakoda

Cauliflower is marinated, dipped in batter, then deep-fried.

Prep - 10 min.   Cook - 15 min.   Servings - 3

Ingredients

To simmer,

- 14 oz. (400 gm.) cauliflower, cut into florets
- 1/2 teaspoon salt
- 3 cups water

To prepare marinade,

- 1 tablespoon minced green chili
- 1 tablespoon ginger-garlic paste
- 1 tablespoon lemon juice
- 1 tsp Kashmiri red chili powder
- 1/4 teaspoon turmeric powder
- 1/2 teaspoon cumin powder
- 1/2 teaspoon coriander powder
- 1/2 teaspoon salt (adjust to taste)
- 1/4 teaspoon black pepper
- 1/2 teaspoon garam masala

To prepare the batter,

- 1 cup chickpea flour
- 2 tablespoons rice flour
- 1/2 teaspoon carom seeds
- 1/2 teaspoon turmeric powder
- 1/4 teaspoon baking soda
- 1/4 cup freshly chopped cilantro
- 1/2 teaspoon salt
- 1/2 cup water

To deep fry,

- Vegetable/neutral oil

Instructions

Step A : Simmer the cauliflower

1. Set a saucepan over medium heat. Add 3 cups of water + 1/2 teaspoon salt, then bring it to a simmer. Then add cauliflower florets and cover the pan. Simmer for 4-5 min, or until they're soft. Drain and set aside to cool.

Step B : Prepare the marinade + batter

2. Mix all the marinade ingredients in a large mixing bowl. Transfer the simmered florets to the bowl. Mix, coat, and let it marinate for 10-15 min.

3. Add all the batter ingredients to a separate large mixing bowl. Stir and mix for 1-2 min, or until the batter has a thick flowing consistency.

Step C : Fry

4. Set a frying pan over high heat. Add oil (the oil has to be at least 2-inches from the bottom of the pan). Once it's hot, turn down the heat to medium.

5. Dip each marinated floret in the prepared batter and then drop it in the pan. Fry for 2 minutes, or until golden brown. Repeat the same for the rest of the florets (do this in multiple batches). Do not overcrowd the pan.

6. Drain on paper towel. Your Gobi Pakoda is ready to serve. Enjoy these delicious snacks with ketchup or imli chutney. Serve with ketchup or imli chutney.

Samosa Pockets

Savory pastry filled with spiced potatoes.

Prep - 15 min.   Cook - 25 min.   Makes - 12 samosas

Ingredients

- 2 cups boiled and mashed potatoes
- 1/2 cup chopped onion
- 1/2 cup chopped green peas
- 2 to 3 green chilies, chopped
- 3 tablespoons chopped cashews
- 3 tablespoons chopped raisins
- 2 tablespoons vegetable oil
- 1 teaspoon cumin seeds
- 1 teaspoon ginger paste
- 1 teaspoon garlic paste
- 1/2 teaspoon turmeric powder
- 1/2 teaspoon red chili powder
- 1/2 teaspoon coriander powder
- Salt to taste
- 24 readymade samosa pastry sheets

Instructions

Step A : Simmer the potato filling

1. In a pan, heat 2 tablespoons of vegetable oil and cumin seeds. Let them splutter.

2. Add 1/2 cup chopped onion and sauté until translucent.

3. Add 1 teaspoon each of ginger paste and garlic paste + chopped green chilies. Sauté for 20-30 seconds.

4. Add 1/2 cup chopped green peas and cook for 2-3 minutes.

5. Add chopped cashews and raisins and cook for another 1-2 minutes.

6. Add turmeric powder, red chili powder, and coriander powder, and salt to taste. Mix well.

7. Add 2 cups of boiled and mashed potatoes and mix everything together.
    Cook for 5-7 minutes, stirring occasionally.

8. Remove the filling from the heat and let it cool down.

Step B : Prepare the sheets (and fill in the potatoes)

9. Take two readymade pastry sheets and overlap them to form a plus sign (+) shape.
    Use a little water to seal the overlapping parts.

10. Place 2 to 3 tablespoons of the filling in the center of this 'plus' sign.

11. Apply a touch of water on the edges of the sheets. Fold one side of the pastry sheet
    over the filling, pressing down on the edges to seal.

12. Fold the opposite side of the other pastry sheet over the filling and press down on
    the edges to seal.

13. Repeat the same process for the other two sides, forming a square-shaped samosa.

14. Place the samosas on the baking sheet and brush them with oil.

15. Bake the samosas in the preheated oven for 18-22 minutes at 375°F (190°C),
    or until they turn golden brown.

16. Samosa pockets are ready. Serve hot with your favorite chutney or sauce.

    Super light and savory snack made with puffed rice (rice puffs).
Prep - 2 min.   Servings - 2

Ingredients

- 1/2 cup chopped cucumber
- 1/2 cup chopped carrot
- 1 large potato, boiled and chopped
- 1/2 cup cooked yellow peas
- 1 onion, chopped
- 1/2 cup chopped tomatoes
- 1/2 teaspoon black salt
- 1 teaspoon roasted cumin powder
- 1 green chili, chopped
- 1/4 teaspoon chili flakes
- 1 tablespoon lemon juice
- Handful of chopped cilantro
- 2.5 cups puffed rice (rice puffs)

Instructions

1. Add all ingredients (except puffed rice) to a large bowl and mix well.
2. Next, add the puffed rice (adding rice in the later stage retains its crispiness).
3. Give it a gentle stir and serve.

Veggie Cheela

Savory Indian pancakes made with Besan.

Prep - 10 min.   Cook - 25 min.   Makes - 5 cheela

Ingredients

To prepare batter,

- 1 cup besan (Bengal gram flour)
- 1/4 teaspoon turmeric powder
- 1/4 teaspoon baking soda
- 1/2 teaspoon salt
- 1/2 cup water
- 1/2 cup pumpkin puree
- 1/4 cup finely chopped green onion
- 1/2 cup grated carrots
- 1/2 cup finely chopped bell pepper
- 1/4 cup finely chopped beans

To prepare tadka,

- 1 tablespoon oil
- 1 teaspoon mustard seeds
- Pinch of asafoetida

To brush,

- Virgin coconut oil

Instructions

Step A : Prepare the batter

1. Add all the batter ingredients in a large bowl. Mix well until thick.

Step B : Prepare the tadka

2. Set a pan over medium heat. Add oil. Once it's hot, add mustard seeds and let it splutter for 30-40 sec. Add asafoetida and let it sauté for 10-15 sec.
   Pour this tadka onto the mixing bowl. Mix well.

Step C : Cook

3. Set a non-stick pan over medium heat. Ladle about 1/2 cup of batter onto the center of the pan. Spread it around using a spatula.

4. Let it cook for 3 min on one side. Flip and brush the cooked side with a bit of coconut oil. Cook the other side for 2-3 min. Flip and brush this side as well. Cheela is ready! Enjoy with hot sauce.

Aloo Pyaaz Paratha

Potato-onion mixture is stuffed in a bread dough, then cooked.

Prep - 15 min.   Cook - 30 min.   Makes - 5 paratha

Ingredients

To prepare the dough,

- 2 cups whole wheat flour
- 1/2 teaspoon salt
- 1 teaspoon oil
- 3/4 cup water

To prepare the stuffing,

- 3 medium potatoes, peeled, cubed, boiled, and cooled
- 1 green chili, chopped
- 1-inch ginger, grated
- 1 large red onion, finely chopped
- 1/4 cup freshly chopped cilantro
- 1/2 tsp Kashmiri red chili powder
- 1/2 teaspoon coriander powder
- 1/2 teaspoon dried mango powder
- 1 teaspoon salt
- 1/4 teaspoon carom seeds

For dusting,

- 1/2 cup wheat flour

To heat/fry the paratha,

- Coconut oil, or any neutral oil

Instructions

Step A: Prepare the dough

1. In a large bowl, add whole wheat flour + salt. Gradually add water while mixing the ingredients together.

2. Continue kneading (using hands) for 5-6 min, or until the dough becomes smooth and somewhat elastic.

3. Gently coat the dough with oil. Then cover it with a wet towel and let it rest for 10 minutes. In the meantime, let's prepare aloo masala (stuffing).

Step B: Prepare the stuffing

4. In a separate bowl, add all the potato-onion stuffing ingredients.

5. Mash and mix until everything is well-combined. Set aside.

Step C: Roll the dough

6. Divide the dough into 5 equal parts.

7. Lightly dust a dry rolling board using a bit of wheat flour. Place 1 part of the dough on the board and roll it into a thick circle (8 cm in diameter and 1 cm in thickness).

8. Scoop and fill around 3 tablespoons of the potato-onion mixture at the center of each circle.

9. Gently bring the edges of the circle toward the center. Once the stuffing is completely enclosed by the dough, gently press the dough at the center. Then press it at the sides. By now the diameter of the circle should be around 10 cm.

10. Place it on a flat, smooth surface. Then lightly dust both sides of the circle with wheat flour.

11. Using a rolling pin, roll it gently into a flat bread of 5 mm thickness and around 15 cm in diameter. While rolling, make sure you roll it from the sides and not from the center. This prevents the paratha from cracking at the edges.

Step D: Heat the paratha

12. Set a skillet over medium heat and place the rolled paratha on it.

13. Heat it for 2 minutes. Flip and heat the other side for 2 more minutes.

14. Pour 1 teaspoon of coconut oil on top and coat well.

15. Flip and pour additional 1 teaspoon coconut oil on the other side. Cook for 1-2 minutes on each side, or until the paratha is golden brown.

16. Aloo pyaaz paratha is ready. Serve hot with chutney, achar, or raita.

Gobi Paratha   Spiced grated cauliflower is stuffed in a bread and cooked.

Prep - 15 min.   Cook - 30 min.   Makes - 5 paratha

Ingredients

To prepare the dough

- 2 cups whole wheat flour
- 1/2 teaspoon salt
- 1 teaspoon oil
- 3/4 cup water

To prepare gobi stuffing

- 2 cups grated cauliflower
- 1/2 teaspoon salt
- 2 green chilies, chopped
- 1/4 cup freshly chopped cilantro

- 1/2 teaspoon dried mango powder
- 1-inch ginger, grated
- 1/4 teaspoon turmeric powder
- 1/4 tsp Kashmiri red chili powder
- 1/4 teaspoon cumin powder
- 1/4 teaspoon coriander powder
- 1/4 teaspoon carom seeds

For dusting,

- 1/2 cup wheat flour

To heat/fry the paratha,

- Coconut oil, or any neutral oil

Instructions

Step A: Prepare the dough

1. In a large bowl, add whole wheat flour + salt. Gradually add water while mixing the ingredients together.

2. Continue kneading (using hands) for 5-6 min, or until the dough becomes smooth, and somewhat elastic. Gently coat the dough with oil. Then cover it with a wet towel and let it rest for 10 minutes. In the meantime, let's prepare the stuffing.

Step B: Remove the moisture from grated cauliflower

3. In a large bowl, add grated cauliflower + 1/2 teaspoon salt. Mix well, cover, and set aside for 20 minutes.

4. *After 20 minutes* Transfer the cauliflower to a strainer. Using the back of a spoon, press and squeeze out the liquid/moisture. Discard the liquid and transfer the cauliflower back to the bowl. Set aside.

Step C: Prepare the cauliflower stuffing

5. To the grated cauliflower bowl, add chilies + cilantro + dried mango powder + ginger + turmeric powder + Kashmiri red chili powder + cumin powder + coriander powder + carom seeds. Mix well.

Step D: Stuff and roll the dough

6. Divide the dough into 5 equal portions. Roll each portion into a thick circle (around 8 cm in diameter and 1 cm in thickness).

7. Scoop and fill around 3 tablespoons of the stuffing mixture at the center of the circle. Next, Bring the edges of the circle toward the center. Once the stuffing is completely enclosed by the dough, gently press it (the dough) at the center. Then press it at the sides. By now the diameter of the circle should be around 10 cm.

8. Place it on a flat, smooth surface. Then lightly dust both sides of the circle with wheat flour.

9. Using a rolling pin, gently roll it into a flat bread that is about 5 mm thick and 12 cm in diameter. While rolling, make sure you roll it from the sides and not from the center. This prevents the paratha from cracking at the edges.

Step E: Heat the paratha

10. Set a skillet over medium heat. Once it's hot, gently place the rolled paratha and let it heat for 2 minutes. Flip and heat the other side for 2 more minutes.

11. Pour 1 teaspoon of coconut oil on top and spread it out using a spatula.

12. Flip and pour additional 1 teaspoon coconut oil on the other side.

13. Cook for 1-2 minutes on each side, or until the paratha is golden brown.

14. Gobi Paratha is ready! Serve with your fav curry or achar (pickle).

Garlic Naan

Soft and fluffy bread with a delicious garlicky flavor.

Prep - 2 hrs.   Cook - 30 min.   Makes - 6 naan

Ingredients

- 1/2 cup + 2 tbsp warm water
- 1 teaspoon sugar
- 1.5 teaspoons active dry yeast
- 2 cups all-purpose flour
- 1/2 teaspoon salt
- 1.5 tablespoons olive oil
- 6 garlic cloves, minced
- 1 tablespoon nigella seeds
- 2 tbsp freshly chopped cilantro
- Coconut oil, to brush
- 1/2 cup all-purpose flour, for dusting

Instructions

Step A: Activate the yeast

1. In a large bowl, add warm water + sugar + active dry yeast. Stir and let it rest for 15 minutes.

Step B: Prepare the dough

2. (After 15 minutes) Add flour + salt + 1 tablespoon olive oil to the large bowl. Mix well.

3. As the dough starts to come together (it turns into a 'shaggy dough'), transfer it to a rolling board and knead for 5-6 min. By now the dough should be soft, smooth, and springy.

   NOTE : Don't worry about the dough being sticky when you're first kneading it. It'll come together after a while.

4. Transfer it to a bowl and coat it with 1/2 tablespoon olive oil. Cover the bowl and let it rest for at least 2 hours.

5. (After 2 hours) The dough will almost double in size. Divide it into 6 even portions.

6. Sprinkle a rolling board with a bit of flour and place one portion of dough on it. Also sprinkle the dough with a bit of flour.

7. Using a rolling pin, roll the dough into the shape of an oval (aim for a thickness of 7 mm) and sprinkle garlic + cilantro + nigella seeds over it. Give it a gentle roll.

8. Set a heavy-base skillet over high heat. Once it's hot, place the bread and heat for 30-45 seconds, or until air pockets (bubbles) appear on top of the bread.

9. Flip and heat the other side for another 30 seconds. Brush coconut oil over the cooked side. Flip and heat some more.

10. Garlic naan is ready! Serve it with dals, curries, and raita.

 A fermented rice batter is cooked into a thin, flat 'crepe'.

Prep - 20 hrs.   Cook - 15 min.   Servings - 3

Ingredients

To prepare batter,

- 1.5 cups Idli rice / parboiled rice (or simply use basmati rice)
- 1/2 cup urad dal
- 1/4 tsp fenugreek seeds (methi)
- 1.5 cups water, to blend
- Salt, to taste

To prepare potato masala,

- 1 tablespoon coconut oil
- 1 teaspoon mustard seeds
- 8-10 fresh/dried curry leaves
- 1-inch ginger, finely chopped
- 2 green chilies, sliced
- 2 medium onions, sliced
- 1/4 teaspoon turmeric powder
- 3 large potatoes - peeled, chopped, and boiled
- 1/2 tsp Kashmiri red chili powder
- 1/2 teaspoon salt (adjust to taste)
- 1/4 cup freshly chopped cilantro

Instructions

Step A: Soak Rice and Dal

1. Rinse the rice until the water runs clear. Transfer it to a large bowl and add 3 cups of water. Soak overnight.

2. In a separate bowl, add urad dal and fenugreek seeds. Soak overnight.

Step B: Blend

3. Once they're soaked, drain the rice and divide it into 2 equal batches. Transfer 1 batch to a mixer/grinder/blender along with 1/2 cup water, and blend to a fine mixture. Move it to a bowl and set aside.

4. Repeat the same for the remaining batch.

5. Next, drain the urad dal mixture and transfer it to the mixer/grinder/blender
    Add 1/2 cup water and blend until smooth. Combine and mix the rice and urad dal
    mixtures together.

Step C: Ferment

6. Cover and set aside in a warm place for 12 to 20 hours and allow the batter to
    ferment. A fermented batter will have a slightly increased volume and thicker, fluffier
    texture.

7. After 12 hours, add 2 to 3 tablespoons of water and salt to the thick fermented batter.
    Give it a gentle stir.

Step D: Prepare the Potato Masala

8. Once the batter is properly fermented, it's time to make potato masala. Set a pan
    over medium heat.

9. Add oil. Once it's hot, add mustard seeds and let them splutter for 30 to 40 seconds.
    Then add curry leaves, ginger, green chilies, onion, and turmeric powder. Stir and
    sauté for 2 to 3 minutes, or until the onions are softened.

10. Next, add the boiled potato chunks, Kashmiri red chili powder, salt, and cilantro. Stir
    well and cook for 2 minutes. Turn off the heat and mash the potatoes using a potato
    masher. Potato masala is ready.

Step E: Prepare the Dosa

11. Set a pan over medium heat. Once it's hot enough, sprinkle around 2 tablespoons of
    water and wipe it off with a clean kitchen towel (sprinkling water cools down the
    surface of the pan, which helps make the dosa crispy).

12. Pour a ladleful of the batter (around 1/2 cup) into the center of the pan.

13. Using the back of the ladle/spoon, spread the batter in a circle in a swirling motion,
    either clockwise or counterclockwise. Let it heat for 2 to 3 minutes, or until the bottom
    is golden and the edges start to lift from the pan.

14. Add the potato masala (around 1/2 cup) on top and fold or roll the dosa. Transfer to
    a serving platter.

15. Before you start cooking another dosa, sprinkle 2 tablespoons of water on the pan
    and wipe it off using a clean kitchen towel.

16. Serve alongside sambar and coconut chutney.

Roti

Round flatbread made with whole wheat flour.

Prep - 5 min.   Cook - 15 min.   Makes - 10 rotis

Ingredients

- 2 cups wheat flour
- 1/2 cup wheat flour, for dusting
- 3/4 cup water
- 1 teaspoon oil
- Coconut oil, to brush

Instructions

Step A : Knead

1. In a medium bowl, add 1/2 cup wheat flour. Set aside.

2. In a large mixing bowl, add 2 cups wheat flour. Gradually add water (1/4 cup at a time) while mixing the flour.

3. Continue kneading (use hands or knuckles) for 3-4 min, or until the dough becomes smooth and soft.

   Note: If it starts to dry and crack, simply dip your knuckle in a bowl of water and knead for 1-2 min. Gently coat the dough with oil. Cover and let it rest for 10 min.

4. (After 10 minutes) Pull around 3 tablespoons of the dough and roll into a smooth disc using your palms. Place it on a large plate. Repeat the same for the rest of the dough.

5. Dip one disc in the medium bowl (that contains the flour) and coat well.

Step B : Roll

6. Dust a rolling board (or a clean, dry wooden/marble surface) with wheat flour. Place the coated disc and gently press to flatten.

7. Using a rolling pin, roll it into a thin, flat circle of diameter 6-7 inches. Once it's nice and flat, place the rolled-out roti on a large plate. Repeat the same for the remaining dough.

   TIP 1 - Roll it vertically to first make an elongated shape. Then rotate it 90 degrees and again roll vertically to make it a circle.

TIP 2 - If the dough starts sticking on the rolling pin (or rolling board), simply dust it with more flour.

Step C : Heat

8. Set a pan over medium-high heat. Once it's hot, place 1 roti and let it heat for 1 min, or until the bubbles start to appear.

9. Flip and heat the other side for 10-12 sec, or until the bubbles expand.

10. If you're using an open-flame stovetop, place the roti (use tongs) directly over the flame for 3 seconds or until it puffs up. Flip and heat for 3 more seconds.

    If you're using an induction stovetop, you'll have to gently press the sides of the roti (using a folded kitchen towel) for it to puff up.

    NOTE : It's okay if some rotis don't puff up. They'll still be soft.

11. Remove from the heat. Lightly coat each side with coconut oil and transfer to an insulated casserole (bowl). Cover it with a clean kitchen towel. Repeat the same for other rotis.

Kaju Katli

Thin & sweet cashew 'slices'.

Prep - 3 min.   Cook - 15 min.   Makes - 15 slices

Ingredients

- 1 cup cashews (raw, unsalted)
- 1/2 cup sugar
- 1/4 cup water
- 1/2 teaspoon cardamom powder
- 1 tablespoon coconut oil

Instructions

Step A : Powder the cashews

1. In a blender, blend the cashews until powdery, around 20-30 seconds. Don't over blend as it might turn oily. Set aside.

Step B : Prepare the sugar syrup

2. Set a thick, non-stick pan over low heat. Add sugar + water. Stir & dissolve the sugar.

3. Once dissolved, add powdered cashews and stir-cook for 4-5 minutes.

4. Add cardamom powder + coconut oil. Stirring continuously, cook for 6- 7 min, or until the mixture starts to thicken and come together.

5. Turn off the heat and transfer the mixture to a parchment-lined plate. Spread it evenly and let it cool for 5-7 minutes.

6. Once it's cool enough to handle, gently knead the cashew 'dough' for 1-2 minutes. Kneading makes the katli consistent in texture.

7. Gently press the dough against the plate and place a large piece of parchment paper on top.

Step C : Roll, cut, fridge

8. Using a rolling pin, roll all sides until it reaches the thickness of 4-5 mm.

9. Remove the parchment. Using a knife, cut the dough into square or diamond shapes. Transfer them to your refrigerator and let them cool for at least an hour. Kaju katli is ready. Enjoy!

Gajar Halwa Sweet and juicy carrot pudding.

Prep - 5 min.   Cook - 35 min.   Servings - 3

Ingredients

- 4 cups grated carrots
- 1/2 cup sugar
- 2 cups almond milk
- Pinch of saffron (optional)
- 1/2 teaspoon cardamom powder
- 2 tablespoons of chopped cashews
- 2 tablespoons of chopped almonds
- 2 tablespoons of chopped raisins

Instructions

1. Set a pan over medium heat and add the grated carrots. Stir and sauté for 2 min.
2. Cover the pan and cook for 5-7 min.
3. Add sugar + almond milk + saffron + cardamom. Give it a quick stir.
4. Cover the pan and cook for 20-25 min, or until much of the milk is absorbed and the carrot starts to caramelize.
5. Sprinkle chopped cashews, almonds and raisins. Mix well and cook for 1 min (do not cover) over low heat. Gajar halwa (carrot pudding) is ready!

Gulab Jamun

Sweet potato dough is rolled, fried, and soaked in syrup.

Prep - 10 min.   Cook - 25 min.   Makes - 10 Gulab Jamuns

Ingredients

To prepare the dough,

- 2 cups boiled & grated sweet potatoes
- 2 tablespoons cornstarch
- 3 tablespoons powdered cashew
- 1/4 teaspoon baking soda
- 1/4 teaspoon cardamom powder
- 1 tablespoon coconut oil

To prepare the sugar syrup,

- 2 cups water
- 1.5 cups sugar
- 1.5 teaspoon edible rose water
- 1/4 teaspoon cardamom powder
- 8-10 saffron strands

To shallow fry,

- Neutral Oil

Instructions

Step A : Prepare the dough

1. Combine all the dough ingredients in a large bowl. Mix well until soft. Divide the dough into 10 even portions.

2. Roll each portion into a smooth ball (make sure there aren't any cracks).

Step B : Prepare the sugar syrup

3. Set a large saucepan over medium heat. Add sugar + water.
   Stir well and bring it to a boil.

4. Once the sugar is dissolved & the solution thickens up a bit, turn down the heat to low-medium and let it simmer for 2 min.

5. Add rose water + saffron strands + cardamom powder and give it a quick stir. Remove the saucepan (cover it with a lid), and set aside.

6. Set a thick pan over low-medium heat. Add oil so that it's at least 2 inches (5 cm) deep.

7. Once the oil is hot, gently add 1-2 dough balls. Fry for 30-40 sec (do not stir), or until the outer surface turns light brown.

8. Gently flip & fry for 8-10 min, or until the color changes to dark brown.

9. Once you're used to this frying technique, you can fry more dough (4-5) at the same time.

Step D : Soak the jamun balls

10. Immediately transfer the jamun balls to the sugar syrup. Let them rest for at least 20 minutes.

    NOTE: If the syrup is cold, warm it up, and then add jamun balls into it.

11. Gulab jamun is ready. Serve warm or chilled.

Pista Kulfi

Creamy and delicious cashew-pistachio popsicle.

Prep - 5 min.   Makes - 5 to 6 kulfis

Ingredients

- 1/2 cup raw pistachios
- 1/4 cup raw cashews
- 1/2 tsp cardamom powder
- 1/2 cup powdered sugar
- 1.5 cups coconut cream

Instructions

1. Blend the pistachios + cashews until powdery.

2. Add cardamom powder + sugar + coconut cream to the blender and blend until smooth.

3. Set a saucepan over medium heat. Transfer the blended mixture to the pan. Bring to a boil.

4. As it just starts to boil, turn down the heat to low. Stirring continuously, simmer for 4-5 minutes, or until the mixture thickens up a bit.

5. Turn off the heat and let it cool. Once cooled, pour it into popsicle molds - make sure you only fill 3/4 portion of the mold. Insert a popsicle stick into the center of each mold.

6. Freeze for at least 8 hours, or until it's set.

7. Pop out and serve chilled.

Mango Kulfi

Mango popsicle made with cashews & coconut cream.

Prep - 22 min.   Makes - 5 kulfis

Ingredients

- 2 cups mango puree
- 1 cup cashews (raw, unsalted)
- 1/2 cup coconut cream
- 1/2 cup powdered sugar
- 1/4 tsp cardamom powder

Instructions

1. Soak cashews in warm water for 20 min. Drain and set aside.

2. Blend mango puree + cashews + coconut cream + powdered sugar + cardamom powder in a blender until smooth and creamy.

3. Pour the mixture into popsicle molds - make sure you only fill 3/4 portion of the mold. Insert a popsicle stick into the center of each mold.

4. Freeze for at least 8 hours, or until it's set. Pop them out and enjoy!

Kheer — Sweet & subtly spiced rice pudding.

Prep - 7 min.   Cook - 45 min.   Servings - 2 to 3

Ingredients

- 3/4 cup basmati rice, soaked for 30 min.

- 5 cups almond milk

- 1/4 to 1/2 cup sugar

- 8-10 raw, unsalted cashews, chopped

- 8-10 raw, unsalted almonds, chopped

- 10-15 whole green (or black) raisins

- 1/2 teaspoon cardamom powder

- Pinch of nutmeg powder

Instructions

1. In a large non-stick pot, add soaked (and drained) basmati rice + 4 cups of almond milk. Cover the pot.

2. Set the pot over medium heat for 35 min. Stir frequently.

3. Next, add the remaining 1 cup of almond milk + all the remaining ingredients. Mix well, cover the pot, and simmer for 10 minutes. Turn off the heat. Serve hot, or chilled.

Pro Tip

Did you know that you can also use vermicelli to make kheer?

Simply replace the rice with an equal amount of vermicelli, a thin noodle-like pasta, in the recipe. The rest of the ingredients and the cooking method can remain the same.

This will give your kheer a thinner and more delicate texture than that of rice. Keep in mind that vermicelli cooks faster than rice, so you might need to adjust the cooking time accordingly.

Sesame Laddoo

4-ingredient dessert made with toasted sesame seeds.

Prep - 5 min.   Cook - 10 min.   Makes - 12 laddoos

Ingredients

- 2 cups raw, white sesame seeds
- 1.5 tablespoons coconut oil
- 1.25 cup jaggery powder
- 1/2 teaspoon cardamom powder

Instructions

1. Set a pan over low-medium heat.
   Add sesame seeds.

2. Stirring continuously, toast the seeds for
   4-5 min, or until they're golden brown.
   Transfer to a bowl and set aside.

3. To the same pan, add coconut oil +
   jaggery powder.

4. Stir and cook over low heat for 4-5 min,
   or until the jaggery is completely melted
   and the mixture starts to thicken (stir
   continuously to prevent jaggery from
   burning).

5. Turn down the heat to low and add the toasted sesame seeds + cardamom powder.
   Stir well until all the sesame seeds are coated with the jaggery.

6. Turn off the heat and transfer to a bowl. Let it cool for 2 minutes.

7. Scoop around 2 tablespoons of the hot sesame mixture and, using wet hands to
   prevent sticking, carefully roll into a ball.

8. Allow the balls to cool and set for at least 30 minutes before serving.
   You can also store them (sealed, in the fridge) for up to a week.

Coconut Laddoo

Sweet, soft, spiced coconut balls/bites.

Prep - 5 min.   Cook - 15 min.   Makes - 12 laddoos

Ingredients

- 2 cups shredded or desiccated coconut (unsweetened)
- 2 cups almond milk
- 3/4 cup sugar
- 3 tablespoons finely chopped almonds
- 1/2 teaspoon cardamom powder

Instructions

1. Set a pan over medium heat. Add shredded coconut + almond milk.

2. Stirring continuously, cook for 8-10 min, or until the coconut has completely absorbed the milk.

3. Add sugar. Stirring continuously, cook for 4-5 minutes, or until the coconut is soft and fluffy.

4. Next, add almonds + cardamom powder. Mix well and cook for 2 min.

5. Turn off the heat and let it cool for 20 minutes.

6. Once it's cooled, dip your hand in a bowl of water and start rolling the coconut mixture into balls about the size of a golf ball (or your preferred size). Repeat the same for the remaining coconut mixture.

7. (Optional) Refrigerate the laddoos for 30 minutes to help them hold their shape before serving.

Besan Laddoo

Besan is roasted, mixed w/sugar and rolled into balls.

Prep - 5 min.   Cook - 15 min.   Makes - 12 laddoos

Ingredients

- 1/2 cup coconut oil
- 2 cups besan (Bengal gram flour)
- Pinch of turmeric powder
- 1/2 teaspoon cardamom powder
- 1 cup powdered sugar
- 10-12 cashews, finely chopped
- 10-12 almonds, finely chopped

Instructions

1. Set a non-stick sauce pan over medium heat. Add oil.

2. Once it's warm, add besan. Stirring continuously, cook for 18-20 minutes, or until the mixture turns paste-like and oily.

3. Turn off the heat, add turmeric powder, and give it a good mix.

4. Transfer to a large bowl, and let it cool for 8-10 min (make sure they're still warm enough to work with).

5. After 8-10 min, add all the remaining ingredients. Mix well using your hands.

6. As you mix, the mixture will gradually turn crumbly and then sticky. Once you achieve this texture, scoop about 2 tablespoons of the mixture and roll it into a sphere. Repeat the same for the remaining mixture.

7. Besan laddoo is ready. Let it cool further for about half an hour (or you can simply freeze them. You can store the laddoos (air-tight) for about 4-5 days.

Banana Lassi

Sweet and tangy banana smoothie.

Prep - 2 min.   Serves - 2 to 3

Ingredients

- 4 ripe bananas - sliced and frozen
- 1 cup soy (or coconut) yogurt
- 1.5 cups almond milk
- 1/4 teaspoon cardamom powder
- 4-5 saffron strands, optional
- 2 tablespoons sugar (adjust to taste)
- 1 tablespoon chopped almonds
- 1 tablespoon chopped cashews
- 1 tablespoon chopped pistachios

Instructions

1. Blend frozen bananas + yogurt + almond milk + cardamom powder + saffron + sugar in a blender.

2. Garnish with chopped nuts and serve chilled.

Mango Lassi

Sweet and tangy mango smoothie.

Prep - 4 min.   Serves - 3

Ingredients

- 2 cups ripe mangoes (peeled, cubed, and frozen)
- 1 cup soy (or coconut) yogurt
- 1.5 cup almond milk
- 1/4 teaspoon cardamom powder
- 2 tablespoons sugar
- 1 tablespoon chopped almonds
- 1 tablespoon chopped cashews
- 1 tablespoon chopped pistachios

Instructions

1. Blend frozen mangoes + yogurt + almond milk + cardamom powder + sugar in a blender.

2. Garnish with chopped nuts and serve chilled.

Imli Chutney   Tangy condiment made from tamarind, jaggery, and spices.

Prep - 5 min.   Cook - 25 min.   Makes - 1 cup

Ingredients

- 1 tablespoon neutral oil
- 1 teaspoon cumin seeds
- 1 teaspoon ginger paste (use mortar-pestle)
- 1/2 tsp Kashmiri red chili powder
- Pinch of asafoetida
- 1/2 teaspoon garam masala
- 2 cups water
- 1 cup jaggery powder (or sugar)
- 3 tablespoons tamarind paste

Instructions

1. Set a thick-bottomed saucepan over low-medium heat. Add oil.

2. Once it's hot, add cumin seeds+ ginger paste + Kashmiri red chili powder + asafoetida + garam masala. Stir and sauté for 1 min.

3. Add water + jaggery + tamarind paste. Stir and mix.

4. Bring the mixture to a simmer. Turn down the heat to low and let it simmer for 20-25 minutes, or until the mixture is thick enough to coat the back of a spoon (stir continuously as it's simmering).

5. Turn off the heat and let it cool. The chutney will thicken more as it cools.

6. You can store the chutney in an airtight container and keep it in the fridge for about 1 week.

> ### Note
>
> For the best results, make sure to use a saucepan with a thick or heavy base as there is a greater chance of burning the chutney when it thickens.
>
> To achieve an authentic flavor in your Imli Chutney, use jaggery powder instead of regular sugar.

Coconut Chutney

Condiment made from grated coconut + spices.

Prep - 10 min.   Cook - 3 min.   Makes - 1.5 cups

Ingredients

To prepare chutney base,

- 1 cup freshly chopped coconut (skin peeled)
- 1-inch ginger
- 2 tablespoons roasted chana dal
- 1/2 teaspoon salt (adjust to taste)
- 2 green chilies
- 1 cup water

To prepare tadka,

- 1 tablespoon oil
- 1/2 teaspoon cumin seeds
- 1/2 teaspoon mustard seeds
- 2 whole dried red chilies
- 1 tablespoon urad dal
- 8-10 fresh/dried curry leaves
- Pinch of asafoetida

Instructions

Step A : Prepare the chutney base

1. Add all the chutney ingredients in a blender and blend well. Set aside in a bowl.

Step B : Prepare the tadka

2. Set a pan over medium heat. Add oil. Once it's hot, add cumin seeds + mustard seeds. Let it splutter for 30- 40 seconds.

3. Add red chilies + urad dal + curry leaves + asafoetida. Stir-sauté for 1- 2 min, or until urad dal turns golden.

4. Pour tadka over the chutney & mix. Coconut chutney is ready!

Tomato Chutney

Spicy condiment made from tomatoes.

Prep - 5 min.   Cook - 15 min.   Makes - 1.5 cups

Ingredients

- 1 tablespoon oil
- 1/2 teaspoon cumin seeds
- 1/2 teaspoon mustard seeds
- 1-inch ginger, grated
- 4 garlic cloves, grated
- 1 onion, chopped
- 8-10 curry leaves (fresh or dried)
- 4 large tomatoes, chopped
- 1/2 teaspoon turmeric powder
- 1/2 teaspoon cumin powder
- 1/2 teaspoon coriander powder
- 1/2 tsp Kashmiri red chili powder
- 1/2 teaspoon salt (adjust to taste)
- 1 teaspoon jaggery powder (or sugar)
- 1/4 cup water
- 1/4 cup freshly chopped cilantro

Instructions

1. Set a pan over medium heat. Add oil. Once it's hot, add cumin seeds + mustard seeds and let them splutter for 30-40 sec.

2. Add ginger + garlic + onion + curry leaves. Stir-sauté for about 3-4 min, or until the onion is golden.

3. Next, add the tomatoes + turmeric powder + cumin powder + coriander powder + Kashmiri red chili powder + salt. Stir well, cover the pan, and cook for 5-6 minutes, or until the tomatoes are wilted.

4. Next, add jaggery powder (or sugar) + water. Stir well, cover the pan, and cook for 5-6 minutes, or until most of the liquid has been absorbed and the chutney has thickened.

5. Turn off the heat. Stir in the freshly chopped cilantro. Tomato chutney is ready!

Mint Chutney

Quick and easy chutney made from fresh mint leaves.

Prep - 5 min.   Makes - 1/2 cup

Ingredients

- 1 cup fresh mint leaves
- 1/2 cup fresh cilantro leaves
- 3 green chilies
- 1/2 teaspoon salt (adjust to taste)
- 1 tablespoon lemon juice
- 2 garlic cloves
- 1/4 cup water
- Pinch of roasted cumin powder
- Pinch of coriander powder
- Pinch of black pepper powder
- 1/4 teaspoon dried mango powder (amchur)

Instructions

1. Blend all the ingredients in a blender until smooth. You can store the chutney in the fridge for 2-3 days.

How to use chutneys

Chutneys are a versatile condiment that can add a burst of flavor to any dish. They can be used as a dip for samosas or as a spread on sandwiches.

You can also mix chutneys with vegan yogurt or mayo to create a delicious dressing for salads. Feel free to experiment and try different chutneys with your favorite dishes to discover new flavor combinations.

Cucumber Achar

Spicy & crunchy 'pickle' made from cucumber & potato.

Prep - 10 min.   Cook - 15 min.   Servings - 4

Ingredients

- 3 medium cucumbers
- 2 large potatoes
- 1 large onion, sliced
- 1/4 cup sesame seeds
- 1/4 cup freshly chopped cilantro
- 2 tablespoons lemon juice
- 1/2 tsp Kashmiri red chili powder
- 1/2 teaspoon salt (adjust to taste)
- 3 tablespoons oil
- 1/8 teaspoon fenugreek seeds
- 2 green chilies, slit lengthwise
- 1/4 teaspoon turmeric powder

Instructions

1. Cut the cucumber vertically into two equal halves. Using a spoon, scoop and remove the seeds and watery 'flesh' from both halves.

2. Slice the halves into bite-sized pieces and transfer them to a large mixing bowl. Set aside.

3. Peel and cut potatoes into bite-sized pieces. Boil for 10-15 min, or until fork-tender. Drain and transfer them to the large mixing bowl.

4. Set a pan over medium heat. Add sesame seeds and stir-roast for 3-4 minutes, or until they're golden brown. Transfer the roasted sesame seeds to a blender and blend in short bursts until powdery.

5. Add the powdered sesame + cilantro + lemon juice + Kashmiri red chili powder + salt to the large mixing bowl. Mix well and set aside.

6. Set a pan over medium heat. Add oil. Once it's hot, add fenugreek seeds + green chilies. Sauté for 30- 40 sec, or until the fenugreek seeds turn dark.

7. Add turmeric powder and stir-sauté for about 10 seconds. Turn off the heat and pour this mixture on top of the large mixing bowl. Mix well. Cucumber achar is ready!

Raita   Spiced & savory condiment made with vegan yogurt.

Prep - 5 min.   Servings - 2

Ingredients

- 14 oz. (400 gm.) cucumber, grated
- 1/4 cup fresh mint leaves, minced
- 1 tablespoon lemon juice
- 1/4 teaspoon coriander powder
- 1/4 tsp roasted cumin powder
- 1.5 cup soy yogurt
  (or use coconut yogurt)
- Pinch of black pepper powder
- 1/2 teaspoon salt (adjust to taste)

Instructions

1. Lightly squeeze the grated cucumber and remove the excess water. Transfer to a mixing bowl.

2. Add all the ingredients (except salt) to the bowl. Mix well and refrigerate for about 1-2 hours. Season with salt and serve.

> ### Note
>
> Raita is typically served as a cooling accompaniment to spicy Indian dishes like curries. The cool and creamy texture of raita helps to balance the heat and spiciness of the main dish, making it a refreshing and satisfying addition to any meal.
>
> Raita is also a healthy and nutritious dish as it is rich in probiotics, which aid in digestion, and essential vitamins and minerals.

Garam Masala

A blend of powdered spices that adds flavors to a dish.

Prep - 2 min.   Cook - 3 min.

Ingredients

- 1/2 cup coriander seeds
- 1/4 cup cumin seeds
- 1 tablespoon fennel seeds
- 10 green cardamom pods
  (cracked open and skin removed)
- 5 black cardamom pods
  (cracked open and skin removed)
- 3 bay leaves
- 7 cloves
- 2 cinnamon sticks
- 2 star anise
- 2 mace strands
- 1 whole nutmeg,
  broken down using mortar-pestle
- 1 teaspoon black peppercorns

Instructions

1. Set a pan over low-medium heat and add all the ingredients.

2. Stirring continuously, roast for 2-3 min, or until aromatic.

3. Turn off the heat and transfer the spices to a spice grinder / blender. Blend in short bursts until powdery.

4. Store in an airtight container in a cool, dark place. It stays fresh for 2 months.

Note

If you're short on time or don't have all the necessary spices on hand, buying pre-made garam masala from a store can be a convenient option.

Most grocery stores carry garam masala, and it can usually be found in the spice aisle.

Keep in mind that different brands may have varying levels of spiciness and flavor intensity. When using store-bought garam masala, start with a small amount and adjust to your taste.

Masala Chai Spice

A blend of powdered spices to make masala chai.

Prep - 2 min.

Ingredients

- 1/2 cup green cardamom pods
- 2 tablespoons cloves
- 1 teaspoon fennel seeds
- 1 tablespoon black peppercorns
- 2 cinnamon sticks (2 in. / 5 cm. each)
- 1 tablespoon ginger powder

Instructions

1. Blend all the ingredients in a spice grinder or blender until powdery.

2. Store in an air-tight container for up to 2 months.

Masala Chai

Classic Indian 'white' tea.

Prep - 3 min.   Cook - 4 min.   Servings - 2

Ingredients

- 1.25 cup water
- 1 teaspoon loose tea leaves
- 3 tablespoons sugar
- 3/4 cup soy milk *
- 1/2 to 1 teaspoon masala chai spice

Instructions

1. Set a pan over medium heat. Add water + tea leaves + sugar.

2. Bring to a boil. Then add soy/almond milk + masala chai spice.

3. Bring down the heat to a low-medium (and simmer for 1 min) Masala chai is ready. Enjoy!

* Note

Plant-based milk like almond milk, rice milk, and oat milk may curdle when making Masala Chai because of their lower fat and protein content.

Paanch Furan Mixture of 5 aromatic seeds that are fried in oil for flavor.
Prep - 1 min.

Ingredients

- 2 tablespoons black mustard seeds
- 2 tablespoons cumin seeds
- 2 teaspoons fenugreek seeds
- 2 tablespoons nigella seeds
- 2 tablespoons fennel seeds

Instructions

1. Combine all ingredients and store it in an airtight container. You can store it in a cool place for months.

How to use Paanch Furan? (Stir-Fried Green Beans Recipe)

Ingredients

- 450 gm. / 1 lb. fresh green beans, trimmed & cut into 1-inch pieces
- 2 tablespoons vegetable oil
- 1 teaspoon Paanch Furan spice blend
- 1/2 teaspoon turmeric
- 1/2 teaspoon red chili powder
- Salt to taste

Instructions

1. Heat the oil in a large skillet or wok over medium-high heat. Once it's hot, add the Paanch Furan. Let it splutter for 30 sec or until fragrant.

2. Add the green beans and stir-sauté for 2 minutes.

3. Add the turmeric + red chili powder + salt and stir well.

4. Reduce the heat to medium and cook the green beans for 5-7 min or until tender but still crisp.

5. Serve hot as a side dish or as a main dish with rice or bread.

Fruit Custard

Creamy and fruity dessert.

Prep - 7 min.   Servings - 6

Ingredients

- 1 cup oat milk (or almond milk)
- Pinch of saffron (~ 20 threads)
- 3 bananas, sliced
- 1/2 teaspoon cardamom powder
- 1 cup coconut cream
- 1 cup sweetened and condensed coconut milk (or condensed oat milk)
- Kiwi, chopped
- Mango, chopped
- Dragonfruit, chopped
- Grapes, chopped
- Pomegranate
- Or your fav fruit

Instructions

1. Heat oat milk (or almond milk) over low heat, until it's just lukewarm.

2. Turn off the heat and add a pinch of saffron. Give it a quick stir and let it sit for 30-40 minutes.

3. Transfer the saffron-infused milk to a blender. Add bananas + cardamon powder, and blend until smooth.

4. Transfer the blended mixture to a large mixing bowl. Add coconut cream + condensed coconut milk (or condensed oat milk). Stir and mix.

5. Now add the chopped fruits: kiwi + mango + dragonfruit + grapes + pomegranate. Mix some more.

6. Cover the bowl and let it chill overnight in your refrigerator.

7. Give your chilled fruit custard a quick stir and transfer to serving bowls. Enjoy!

Chutney Sandwich

Cilantro and mint chutney is spread on a sandwich bread.

Prep - 12 min.   Cook - 7 min.   Servings - 2

Ingredients

To prepare green chutney,

- 2 cups cilantro (lightly packed)
- 1 cup mint (lightly packed)
- 1-inch piece ginger (roughly chopped)
- 3 green chilies (use 1-2 for less heat)
- 1.25 teaspoons salt
- 1/2 teaspoon pepper
- 1 teaspoon cumin seeds
- 3 tbsp roasted chickpea flour (sattu)
- 4 tablespoons lemon juice
- 2 tablespoons water

To fry tofu,

- 1 tablespoon olive oil
- 200 gm./ 7 oz. firm tofu, sliced into 8 pieces
- Salt and pepper

To toast the bread,

- 2 sandwich bread slices
- 1 tablespoon olive oil

To assemble,

- Vegan mayonnaise, lettuce, onion, tomato

Instructions

Step A : Prepare the green chutney

1. In a blender/grinder, add all the chutney ingredients and blend until saucy. Set aside.

Step B : Fry the tofu slices

2. Set a pan over medium heat. Add olive oil. Once it's hot, sprinkle salt + pepper and add the tofu slices. Fry for 2-3 min, until golden. Flip & fry the other side for 2-3 min.

Step C : Toast the bread

3. Set the (same) pan over medium heat. Add oil. Once it's hot, add the sandwich bread and toast until golden brown. Turn off the heat and set aside.

Step D : Assemble

4. Pour and slather 2 sandwich slices with vegan mayo and green chutney.

5. Layer the mayo-slathered slice with lettuce, tomato slices, salt (sprinkle a pinch of salt on top of tomato slices), fried tofu slices, and sliced onion. Finally, place the chutney-slathered slice on top and press. Chutney sandwich is ready. Enjoy!